The Complete Guide to

Selling Stocks Short

Everything You Need to Know
Explained Simply

By Matthew G. Young

THE COMPLETE GUIDE TO SELLING STOCKS SHORT: EVERYTHING YOU NEED TO KNOW EXPLAINED SIMPLY

Library of Congress Cataloging-in-Publication Data

Young, Matthew G.
 The complete guide to selling stocks short : everything you need to know explained simply? / by Matthew G. Young.
    p. cm.
 Includes bibliographical references and index.
 ISBN-13: 978-1-60138-326-6 (alk. paper)
 ISBN-10: 1-60138-326-6 (alk. paper)
 1. Short selling. 2. Stocks. 3. Speculation. I. Title.
 HG6041.Y678 2010
 332.63'228--dc22

                                        2010017423

PROJECT MANAGER: Shannon McCarthy • PEER REVIEWER: Marilee Griffin
INTERIOR DESIGN: Samantha Martin
FRONT & BACK COVER DESIGN: Jacqueline Miller • millerjackiej@gmail.com

Printed on Recycled Paper

Printed in the United States

We recently lost our beloved pet "Bear," who was not only our best and dearest friend but also the "Vice President of Sunshine" here at Atlantic Publishing. He did not receive a salary but worked tirelessly 24 hours a day to please his parents. Bear was a rescue dog that turned around and showered myself, my wife, Sherri, his grand-

parents Jean, Bob, and Nancy, and every person and animal he met (maybe not rabbits) with friendship and love. He made a lot of people smile every day.

We wanted you to know that a portion of the profits of this book will be donated to The Humane Society of the United States. *–Douglas & Sherri Brown*

The human-animal bond is as old as human history. We cherish our animal companions for their unconditional affection and acceptance. We feel a thrill when we glimpse wild creatures in their natural habitat or in our own backyard.

Unfortunately, the human-animal bond has at times been weakened. Humans have exploited some animal species to the point of extinction.

The Humane Society of the United States makes a difference in the lives of animals here at home and worldwide. The HSUS is dedicated to creating a world where our relationship with animals is guided by compassion. We seek a truly humane society in which animals are respected for their intrinsic value, and where the human-animal bond is strong.

Want to help animals? We have plenty of suggestions. Adopt a pet from a local shelter, join The Humane Society and be a part of our work to help companion animals and wildlife. You will be funding our educational, legislative, investigative and outreach projects in the U.S. and across the globe.

Or perhaps you'd like to make a memorial donation in honor of a pet, friend or relative? You can through our Kindred Spirits program. And if you'd like to contribute in a more structured way, our Planned Giving Office has suggestions about estate planning, annuities, and even gifts of stock that avoid capital gains taxes.

Maybe you have land that you would like to preserve as a lasting habitat for wildlife. Our Wildlife Land Trust can help you. Perhaps the land you want to share is a backyard—that's enough. Our Urban Wildlife Sanctuary Program will show you how to create a habitat for your wild neighbors.

So you see, it's easy to help animals. And The HSUS is here to help.

2100 L Street NW • Washington, DC 20037 • 202-452-1100
www.hsus.org

Dedication

This book would not have happened without the help of my two superb editors, Erin Everhart and Shannon McCarthy. Their help and attention to the many details of a complicated topic was more than any writer should ever ask of his or her editors.

My family was amazingly patient during the course of the writing of this book as well. My lovely wife, Beth, was neglected for many hours on end while I was in front of the computer typing. I also owe my mother Helen a big thank you for letting me use her computer and its cord whenever I needed them.

Thank you also to my case study participants. The book would not be complete without your expertise and help.

Table of Contents

Chapter 2:
An Introduction to Selling Stocks Short   55

Chapter 3:
What You Need to Begin   73

Chapter 4:
When to Short a Position   89

Chapter 9:
Put Options   199

Chapter 10:
Exit Strategies   221

Chapter 11:
Testing the Waters   235

Table of Contents

Introduction

Selling Short as a Regular Trading Practice

S elling stocks short is usually a taboo subject. When U.S. markets performed poorly in the past, whether you look back to the Great Depression that began in October of 1929 or the most recent crash of 2008, selling short was blamed — at least to some extent. The practice was even banned for almost 800 companies for a few weeks in the midst of the 2008 crash. So why would anyone want to partake in such a heinous act?

This question begs another: *Is selling short actually that bad?*

Short selling, in the most literal sense, involves borrowing the shares of a company and then immediately selling them. The shares of stock must be returned eventually, so the second part of selling short involves buying the stocks back and returning them to the broker they were borrowed from. Essentially, this is the exact opposite of how the market usually works. The mechanics are the same as any traditional trade: You want to buy low and sell high. But the order in which the components take place is reversed in an ideal trade; short sellers will first sell high and then buy low. You are, as a short seller, hoping that markets will decline in price.

In the eyes of the market, though, short selling carries out the same function as a traditional long sale, and it makes no difference to brokers whether you have a long or a short position as long as you do not run the risk of not being able to cover your position. The broker will still make money off of your commissions either way. And it does not matter to the overall markets because supply and demand are still vital aspects of a short sale. There has to be two consensual parties to any trade: a buyer and a seller. Again, only the order in which these requirements occur is changed. Supply is created, demand is satiated, and trades are meant to be completed. You do not buy a few shares of a stock with the intent of just giving your money away to a company. You buy stock shares in order to sell them for a profit at some point in the future. Why then has short selling been given such a bad reputation? Stocks are meant to be bought and sold, so does the order in which these actions occur really matter if they affect the market in the same manner?

Short selling has gotten such a bad reputation because it is a practice for contrarians, individuals seeking to gain when stocks go down in price, but there is absolutely no indication that markets suffer due to short selling. In fact, many markets rely on short selling in order to function. As you will see in Chapter 8, this is the case in many of the non-equity sectors, such as the foreign exchange, commodity futures, and the options market. Just like all other trades, this type of trade requires both a buyer and a seller; both parties must be willing to enter into the trade. This further implies that both parties have, or think they have, something to gain from the trade. Short selling is not only an acceptable function of these markets, it is vital for conducting business. Without both parties becoming involved and hoping to make a profit, trading would cease. Short sales do not occur because only one party wants to make a profit; they happen because there is the potential that the trade will be mutually beneficial to all parties involved.

Short selling works because both of the parties involved come to an agreement. One party believes that the stock in question will rise, while the other thinks that the price will fall. In effect, this is a consensual exchange that fulfills the two vital market roles: buying and selling, regardless of what type of trade is being conducted.

This does not mean that short selling is for everyone. Many successful traders have never shorted a stock throughout their illustrious careers. Because of this, short selling is more than a little misunderstood. Over the years, there have even been some attempts at restricting short sellers, even going as far as outright banning the practice. Most of the general rules associated with the stock market today arose as a reaction to the Great Depression. The Securities and Exchange Commission (SEC) was created, and alongside it, so were many regulations. One of these laws was the uptick rule, which basically stated that a short sale could only take place on a rising stock. In effect, it made it impossible to short sell a falling stock. This rule, thankfully, was abandoned in 2007, although many traders are still not aware of this. While this might seem counter-intuitive, it is a good indicator of the public's sentiment regarding selling short. In theory, the rule was put in place in order to protect traditional long sellers from people looking to make a quick profit off of a stock while it is in a rapid decline.

Despite improvements to the trading atmosphere, selling short still is not a mainstream practice. In fact, because of the repeal of the uptick rule, many blamed the so-called "Great Recession" that began in 2008 on the new trading conditions that were created once the rule was gone. The argument goes that the market has become more volatile since repealing the uptick rule. On the surface this might appear to be true; the market conditions of 2010 are certainly very different than the market conditions of 2000, but whether the difference is due to fewer restrictions on short selling is debatable. What is not debatable is that the market was overextended and that many key sectors were suffering from inflated prices prior to the crash that occurred in September 2008.

Of course, time will be the deciding factor in settling this question. When the practice of the short selling was banned, the result was minimal at best. In fact, the SEC Chairman at the time, Christopher Cox, commented in December 2008 that the same measures would probably not be used if the SEC knew then what it later learned; in other words, they would not have banned short selling because it did nothing to restore sanity to the markets.

Selling short a stock is still a process clouded in mystery, but because it is so seldom understood, you are giving yourself an edge over many other traders. Unless you are very lucky, without an edge you are going to be faced with average returns, and if you do it long enough you will probably be mirroring that of any given index. This is not necessarily a bad thing; the market has risen by an average of about 3 percent a year since the Great Depression ended. But you would not be reading this book if you were content with just average returns on your investment.

Let selling short be your edge. It is an invaluable tool that allows traders to profit, no matter what the market conditions are. With this extra tool in your arsenal, you will be giving yourself that edge over the millions of other traders who do not understand or are afraid to sell short.

One of the few truisms of the stock market is that stocks fall at a much faster rate than they rise — and stocks always go down, even the major blue chip companies. Oscillation is another truth that describes the stock market. Stock prices fluctuate up and down, much like waves on the ocean, so even when a stock is climbing in price, it does not go straight up. Usually, this oscillation stays within a range called a price channel, and day traders thrive off of these minor changes. By trading large quantities of shares, day traders, both on the long and short side, are able to generate profits from these daily fluctuations.

It is when prices break outside of their range that catches most other traders' attention. When a stock begins falling, traders go through a series of emotions: anxiety, greed, and foolishness are prevalent, but fear is chief amongst them. Many traders will abandon their position, cutting their losses early, hoping they made the right decision. Even more will wait, hoping that the market will rebound quickly so that they may continue making money. A tiny fraction of these traders will even continue to buy more shares, predicting that the market will bounce back up and that the new shares bought will be at a discount. As a short seller, you are given another option. When you think a stock is about to fall, you can merely sell it short and reap in the gains while the stock drops.

It should be noted that there is a big difference between the terms "investor" and "trader." Investors buy stocks and bonds and hold them for long periods of time, usually several years. Traders, on the other hand, hold their stock positions for much shorter periods of time. As a short seller, you are a trader, not an investor, out of necessity for two main reasons:

- The market has an overall upward trend. If you stay short for long periods of time, you are very likely to lose money.

- Brokers simply will not let you borrow their shares for indefinite periods of time.

As a trader, you are looking for short-term gains. Because these gains are usually (but not always) going to be less in gains and more frequent, traders conduct their business with larger amounts of money to avoid slippage and make a profit. There are many more fees that traders will face due to their more frequent activity.

Common market knowledge states that the greater the element of risk, the more lucrative the outcome will be. This is the case with some trades, but it does not need to be for yours. While there are some high-risk trades that might pay off with huge rewards, there are also plenty of low-risk trades with just as profitable ends. Risk can be a double-edged blade, cutting you in two different manners. Not only is there a more probable chance that you can lose money, risk clouds your judgment. When your emotions get involved in a trade and when you feel an attachment to your trading money, you run a much higher chance of making mistakes.

Decision making is a vital part of any trader's arsenal of tools, and the most important aspect is to stay disciplined. Whether it is poor impulse control or letting their emotions take over their judgment, once a trader strays from his or her plan, mistakes are made more often than not. In the stock market, mistakes cost money, and too many will spell certain financial ruin. It is important you make your own decisions. Only you know what type of trading is going to work for you and what type of risk you are able to handle. While there are many cookie-cutter systems out there, you will have to form your own personal method if you wish to be successful. By revisiting your records and identifying both the good and the bad trends within your trading regimen you will make yourself a better trader. If you only adhere to someone else's method, you will never improve.

You have three jobs as a trader: learning from the past, analyzing future trades in light of the past, and then executing them. Sounds simple, right? Think again. Balancing these three tasks can be a difficult process, especially when you take into account the psychological aspect of trading. There is a gap between these jobs and there is plenty of room for error. It is extremely easy to lose your cool when it comes time to follow through on the trade that you have spent hours preparing for.

Rather than trying to think in the heat of the moment, make your job as a trader easier. When it is time to analyze, just analyze. And when it is time to trade, just trade. Make your trading life simpler by taking the thinking out of trade execution. You should have your trades plotted out ahead of time, complete with exit points for both losses and profitable trades. This will eliminate the guesswork that so many traders operate with. Rather than just arbitrarily attacking the stock market, you will have your trades completely outlined and will have a blueprint to work from.

Famous short sellers

Throughout history, short selling has been controversial and lucrative. Many traders have amassed a fortune thanks to short selling. Some of these individuals come with a degree of notoriety, but the fact remains: Short selling can be an extremely beneficial weapon if you know how to properly use it.

Jesse Livermore

Jesse Livermore was an early 1900s stock trader. After the Crash of 1929, Livermore had reportedly earned over $100 million during the Great Depression because of his short selling strategy.

Livermore began his career early by trading in "bucket shops" at age fifteen. A bucket shop was a betting parlor that specialized in bets that mirrored stocks' performances. Although they mimicked a stock's action, there was no actual change in ownership. Eventually, Livermore was banned from the bucket shops because of his prowess. He then moved on to the actual stock market.

Livermore remains an interesting and important character within the trading world. He made and lost several fortunes by straying from his trading plans. This is a great example of why traders need to create and then abide by their rules.

William J. O'Neil

William O'Neil, founder of the *Investor's Business Daily*, was one of the first traders to use computers in his trading strategy. Since then, he has penned several books, including some on short selling. O'Neil is a technical trader, and he relies heavily on chart signals before entering a trade. Computers have made the creation of complex charts an instantaneous action, allowing the technical trader to vastly expand their trading practices. The groundbreaking CAN-SLIM® system is the program that O'Neil created as his contribution to the now high-tech world of trading. O'Neil's company, William O'Neil + Co., Inc., specializes in servicing institutional investors.

Dr. Alexander Elder

Dr. Alexander Elder has written multiple books on selling stocks both long and short. Elder, a former psychiatrist, offers some of the most insightful advice in the trading world through his trading camps and Web seminars. His Web site can be found at **www. elder.com**.

The StockFinder® program offered on Elder's site is one of the most advanced systems out there. This allows traders to not only look at historical charts and information, but it also comes with a trading diary feature, something that will prove to be the backbone of any good trading platform.

Who Should Sell Short?

There are three factors that determine just who selling stocks short will benefit. These three factors must all be met before you begin; if even one of these does not apply to you, stay away from selling short until there is some sort of change:

- Expendable money
- Fortitude
- Knowledge

The first qualification is for individuals with enough expendable income to warrant a riskier short-term allocation of their money. Putting minimum margin account amounts aside, selling short is an expensive practice. In order to see gains, you will need to trade thousands of dollars at a time, in some cases. If you do not feel comfortable with this, do not sell short.

Second, you must have the nerves to accurately fulfill your goals. Short selling can be difficult and, at times, heartbreaking. You will not succeed with every trade. You need to have the gumption to be able to recover your losses and try again.

The third factor is knowledge. If you are not sure of what you are doing, do not sell short. Practice with fake money first, and then ease your way into trading by using miniscule amounts of cash to trade with. You do need real life experience to be a successful short seller; this is the proper way to gain that experience.

If you feel that you have fulfilled each of these three criteria, selling short will be a valuable skill to add to your trading arsenal.

Chapter 1

An Introduction to the
Stock Market

The stock market is a broad term encompassing all markets in which stocks, bonds, and commodities are bought and sold. This can be an actual physical place where such trades are conducted, such as with the New York Stock Exchange (NYSE), where orders are shouted out by the individuals on the trading floor, but it also refers to the virtual marketplace where trades take place via the Internet. Most markets today have become more technologically savvy and use the Internet to facilitate trading.

However, you cannot just start trading on your own; only individuals with a securities license can buy and sell stocks directly. Because of this, you must conduct your trades through a stock brokerage firm. Your broker acts upon orders that you give them and conducts the actual trade for you, at a price of course. There are many varieties out there, ranging from full-service to do-it-yourself. The full-service brokers are titled as such because they will not only conduct trades for you, they will also give you advice and may offer products other than securities, such as insurance.

This book is aimed at getting you past the need for a full-service broker and focuses on teaching you to become a do-it-yourself trader. Whether you aim to become a full-time trader, or you just want to utilize short selling as a money-making hobby, this book will point you in the right direction. The vast majority of the brokers you can use for this purpose can be found on the Internet, allowing you to trade virtually in real-time. Depending on your wants and needs, there are many good online brokers that allow their clients to buy, sell, and sell short. The following are just a few of the most popular sites:

- **ShareBuilder® (www.sharebuilder.com):** ShareBuilder is a discount online broker. There is no minimum needed to open an account; you can trade with as little money as you would like. For a real-time trade, they charge $9.95 per trade. Short sales, because of they are more labor-intensive, cost a bit more.

- **Scottrade (www.scottrade.com):** Scottrade is another discount online broker. They boast automatic trades for as little as $7 per trade. For short sellers, they also offer margin rates at 7.75 percent. Margin accounts, a necessity for short sellers, require an initial deposit of $2,000.

- **E*TRADE (www.etrade.com):** E*TRADE charges $9.99 per trade. For those trading with smaller amounts, they offer a margin rate of 7.99 percent, with a minimum margin account balance of $2,000.

- **Thinkorswim (www.thinkorswim.com):** Thinkorswim specializes in options trading. They charge $2.95 per contract being traded. This site has won multiple awards from Barron's, including No. 1 Overall Online Broker.

Before you are ready to trade online though, a few key terms must be understood. These terms will be covered in the next section. You can also look in the glossary at the back of the book for further definitions.

Stocks, Bonds, and Options

Stocks and bonds are two of the most prominent mainstays within the international market. Stock shares represent a fraction of ownership within a corporation. If there are 100 shares issued for a particular company, and an individual buys 10 of them, then that investor owns 10 percent of that company. There are two ways in which a shareholder may profit. As the company's stock rises in value, the shareholder is entitled to the price difference if he or she sells off the shares. For example, if an investor buys 10 shares of a stock for $10 per share and then the stock rises to $15 per share, that investor may choose to sell their stock for a profit of $50, or $5 for each of the shares owned.

The second way in which a shareholder might make money is if dividends are paid out. A **dividend** is a sum of money that is paid out per share, bypassing the sale of the stock. In other words, investors do not need to sell off their shares in order to net a profit from their holdings. This is an added bonus and allows companies to show their appreciation for long-term investors. If a shareholder owns 10 shares of a stock and there is a profit of $5 per share, the company may choose to pay half of that to each shareholder. The shareholder who owned 10 shares would then receive a check for $25: $2.50 for each of the 10 shares he or she owns. The payment of dividends is not an obligation for corporations and may be paid at the corporation's board of directors' discretion. This usually occurs yearly but can be as frequent as once a quarter.

A **bond**, on the other hand, is a debt that the corporation owes and will repay in the future plus interest. It does not represent any ownership in the company and thus has none of the rights that shareholders possess. Bonds are considered safer investments than stocks because if the company invested in was to go belly-up, bondholders are to be repaid prior to shareholders. Because they are lower-risk instruments, bonds will typically pay a smaller return than stocks. Bonds can be bought directly from a company or from other traders selling them on the open market. They can only be sold short if they are included as part of a fund that does allow short selling, as they are a loan and thus cannot be borrowed.

Options have recently exploded in popularity, especially for those looking to sell short. Sometimes referred to as derivatives, these were first officially traded in the United States in 1982. A call option gives an investor the choice, but not the obligation, to purchase a stock at a given price. Because options traders are trying to predict the future, there is no guarantee as to what the actual price of the stock will be down the road, and thus no guarantee as to whether the trade will end up being profitable. There are two players involved when it comes to options, just as with a traditional sale. The holder is the individual who is given the choice of whether he or she wishes to execute the option. The writer is the party that is going to provide the financial product being offered. Most sites, including thinkorswim, require you to fill out an application prior to trading in options to determine your trading experience and financial solvency. Basically, any application that you fill out is for your safety; they do not want people with little experience or expendable capital to lose their life savings in the options trade.

If the holder wishes to back out of the trade, nothing except the option premium is lost. The writer, on the other hand, can lose quite a bit if prices change drastically. For example, assume that an investor (holder) wanted the opportunity to purchase 10 shares of Green Mountain Coffee Roasters (GMCR) one year from now at $75 per share. If prices drop below $75, the investor will not want to purchase the more expensive option and will back out of their contract. They have not lost anything except the premium that was paid to hold the option open for them. This can range anywhere from a few dollars to a several hundred dollars, depending on the amount of contracts and the price that is desired, and is pure profit for the writer. Typically, one option contract entails 100 shares of the stock in question. If on the other hand, the price of the stock rises to $100 per share, the investor will have the opportunity to purchase the stocks at a discount of $25 per share. If they turned around and then sold the shares immediately, the discount received would be pure profit, minus the premium. If this were to occur, the writer would be at a large loss.

Options are an investment product with much potential for gains if used correctly. *Put options, and how they relate to short selling, will be discussed in greater detail in Chapter 9.*

Basket funds

A basket fund is a generic term for a group of stocks that are placed together in one investment, either because they are similar companies or to gauge the health of a portion of the economy. This term covers mutual funds, indices, and exchange-traded funds (ETFs). All of these are great ways to avoid inflation-related losses since they will more closely mirror the market as a whole than an individual stock would, thus making them important and useful investment products.

Mutual funds: A mutual fund is a pooled investment with many investors' money being combined in order to give the fund manager more leverage than an individual investor could have alone. Mutual funds usually are comprised of companies from many sectors of the market and use their diversification to minimize losses. Mutual funds are characterized by the fact that a fund manager tightly manages them. The fund manager directs which corporations' stocks are included within the fund and to what degree. Mutual funds have the highest cost associated with them because they are so carefully managed. For the vast majority of short sellers, mutual funds are not something they need to be concerned with because they focus more on the long-term.

Indices: An index is a measurement tool within the stock market and is the most widely known aspect of the stock market, as they are often referenced when quoting the overall health of the market or a sector within the market. The Dow Jones Industrial Average (DJIA) is the most famous of these. An index is much more stable than an individual stock because a few stocks within the index can go through a drastic drop, yet if the index is generally spread out, it will mostly sustain its position. A manager does not oversee indices, which gives them a lower cost to own, making them extremely valuable to the short seller.

Exchange-traded funds: An ETF is basket fund of similar stocks. For example, a hypothetical ETF could be comprised of the stock from five oil-processing companies. ETFs are traded just as an individual stock would be; they are grouped together by an ETF sponsor. These sponsors can be corporations or financial institutions. Sponsors are responsible for maintaining and adjusting their own funds. These are relatively new in the American marketplace and are quickly growing in popularity. Beginning in 2008, ETFs were allowed to take the shape of actively managed funds, increasing in their popularity. There are approximately 1,500 ETFs globally.

These are usually used for shorter-term investments. If the ETF owner possesses a large number of shares of a particular fund (usually around 50,000), he or she is given the opportunity to trade the ETF shares in for a representative share of the stocks comprising the ETF. This is particularly useful for investors looking to save on commission fees. ETFs generally have lower costs associated with their buying and selling than stocks do. Rather than having many separate transaction charges for buying so many shares, there would only be one charge for the purchase of the 50,000 shares of the ETF in the above example. *Inverse exchange-traded funds are popular tools for short sellers and will be covered in Chapter 8.*

Foreign exchange

The foreign exchange market is the world's most popular marketplace. Currencies of different nations trade hands whether it is due to a tourist visiting another country or an investor hedging his U.S. stock investment by investing in Japanese Yen. Out of necessity, the foreign exchange market allows people to travel and interact with other countries' economies.

Commonly known as the forex, this marketplace revels in the trading of trillions of dollars daily. It is generally best for new traders to avoid the forex marketplace as its trading conditions have often been likened to gambling. It is sometimes very difficult for an individual to gauge the strength of economies that they do not experience every day on a personal level. Still, there is a science to the trading of currency, albeit an inexact one. Some of the issues dictating price are:

- Gross national product.
- National debt.
- Political science issues.
- Type of economy.

If you are not thoroughly familiar with currency trading and how international issues affect the trade, it is probably for the best that you stay away from this type of trading until you are more confident. Although short sellers can use currency, this topic is very broad and merits a separate book itself. *Currency trading, and how to be successful at it, will be detailed further in Chapter 8.*

Commodities

Almost any tangible item can be traded in both the domestic and international markets. Popular commodities range from pork bellies to diamonds, although oil and coffee are the No. 1 and No. 2 most-traded products, respectively, accounting for several billions of dollars being traded daily.

Commodity futures differ from options with the fact that they are mandatory trades. When you enter a futures position, you are signing a contract that guarantees you will be selling the agreed upon amount of commodities to a buyer. With options, the trade is only executed if you want to execute it. Because of this distinction, commodities have an added degree of risk. Trading commodities is more risky than trading options; until you are a bit more experienced, these types of trades should be delayed due to the fact that you are obligated to fulfill your end of the contract.

The commodity market is normally centralized just as the stock exchanges are. In the United States, the New York Mercantile Exchange acts as the largest forum where commodity trades take place.

With the use of commodity futures, a selling strategy originally used by farmers to guarantee the best prices for their crops and livestock, these tangible goods can be sold short in a similar manner to put options. *How you can use these futures to make a profit without actually having to buy and store hundreds of pork bellies in your home will be discussed in Chapter 8.*

investment
financial
commodity
property
durable
bond
asset
goods
returns
option
speculation
return
becomes
buy
lender
involved
good
sum
economic
gains
provides
liability
exchange
equivalent
bank
organization
pension
period
future
it
income
analyzed
denominated
instrument
economics
management
comes
claim

Types of Stockholders

Although almost anything can be sold short, stocks are the primary focus of this book mainly because the lessons learned from the analysis of the stock market can be carried over to the other types of trading on the stock market.

There are a few different types of people who purchase stocks, but they can mainly be broken down into two main categories: investors and traders. These two categories are defined by the length of time for which they hold the stocks they purchase. An investor will buy a stock and hold it for quite a while, sometimes for several years. For instance, shareholders of IBM might have bought their shares over a decade ago and may be waiting another decade to cash their shares in for retirement capital. These types of investors look for the overall value within their purchase and are not concerned with the daily fluctuations over the short-term. Investors mainly buy the time-tested blue-chip stocks, like IBM, that trade in large volumes. These large cap stocks have withstood the weathering of time and, although they may not increase in value each year, they have proven that they are not going to fold in the foreseeable future and will be profitable over long periods of time. The biggest difference between an investor and a trader is the length of time for which positions, or open trades, are held. With that said, there are three main types of traders.

- **Position trader:** A position trader will usually keep a trade open for a few weeks. These traders look for undervalued stocks that show potential for change and hope to either sell the stock short when its price is relatively high or buy the stock while it is cheap.

- **Swing trader:** Swing traders seldom keep a position open for more than a few days. Because of this, they are required to trade with a larger volume of money than a position trader would. This is due to the fact that the stocks purchased may not change in price as much as a position might that was held for longer. In order to net a profit after commissions and fees are added to their trade, trades should involve at least enough to cover commissions and fees after the trade is completed.

- **Day trader:** Day traders take swing trading one step further by keeping positions open for less than a day. They very rarely keep trades open overnight. In order to make enough money to make a trade worthwhile, very large amounts of money are needed in order to make a profit. Day traders typically use $10,000 or more to trade with at any given time.

Pattern Day Traders

The government has safeguards built into laws regarding the stock market in order to protect corporations from fraud and to help prevent financial ruin for overzealous traders. If you are labeled as a "pattern day trader," you will be required to keep at least $25,000 in your margin account. The pattern day trader is defined as someone who buys and sells a stock within the same day for four out of five days during any given period.

The main types of traders vary by the time that a position is held, the amount of money exchanged per transaction, and the percentage change necessary within the purchased stock's value in order to turn a profit. Because day traders trade in a higher volume than position traders, they can profit off of a change as little as a few cents per share. Position traders need larger differences because they generally use less money for their trades.

It is important not to mix up the types of trade you are conducting. If you are planning on a day trade, and the price you were hoping for does not materialize within the original time period that you allotted for it, do not hold on and make it a long-term trade. The use of a written trading diary will help you prevent this from happening. The danger lies in the planning; if your trades are straying from that plan, it can be a very costly error of judgment.

CASE STUDY: RESEARCH IS THE KEY

Laura Goldman
CEO, LSG Capital

Laura Goldman has been a professional trader since 1981. Currently, she owns her own company, LSG Capital, where she acts as CEO. The goal she has set for her customers is lofty: a 20 percent increase each year. This is not something that is easy, but Goldman tries to achieve this by staying on top of the market by constantly researching new and existing trades. The majority of her day is spent studying up on stocks and distressed bonds through Web sites like TheStreet (**www.thestreet.com**), the Wall Street Journal (**www.online.wsj.com**), and MarketWatch (**www.marketwatch.com**).

Although Goldman targets risk-takers, she does not want her clients to be uneducated. A risk taker, according to Goldman, is someone who is willing to sustain the inevitable losses that will occur when going for larger returns. Her ideal customer is knowledgeable of the stock market so that they can respect and understand the moves she makes with their money. Short selling is a risky maneuver; Goldman wants to make sure that her customers can appreciate the risk since this is oftentimes the only way to secure large returns. Overall, the amount of short and long positions she takes varies depending on the market conditions.

Another key point is that Goldman's clients are mostly word of mouth customers. The majority of her clients have some sort of personal relationship with Goldman, either through her charity work, her writing, or a mutual acquaintance. This level of closeness gives her clients a trust that cannot be bought through advertising.

Goldman is not a day trader. On the contrary, she will hold positions and wait until they hit the target price she has set for them. For example, when the news of fraud within Goldman Sachs came out, she opened a short position within that company, covering it the next trading day, waiting until the bulk of the damage had been done.

And like all other traders, Goldman occasionally faces losses. When these inevitably occur, she will take out her frustrations with exercise. By refreshing her mind through physical exertion, she maintains a level of coolness when trading, allowing her body to work out the stress that has accumulated.

Beginning Trading

In order to survive and prosper within the world of trading, you will need to understand some of the most basic actions involved with trading. When it comes to buying stocks, there are two prices listed, the bid and the ask price. The bid is what traders are willing to pay, and the ask is what companies and other financial institutions are willing to sell their shares for.

The average investor cannot just decide they want to purchase a stock. Purchases must take place through a licensed stockbroker who facilitates the trade for the buyer for a commission. The buying and selling of stocks vary in price depending on the type of broker you use and the type of trade you wish to execute. The most basic trade is the market order buy and sell. The broker conducts the buy or sell within a reasonable time frame at the market price. This usually occurs within a few minutes of the order. Because the trade does not take place instantly, the finalized price may vary depending on how much the stock's price fluctuates between the order and the execution of the trade. With the vast majority of instances, this will only be a few cents difference.

There are ways around the imperfect market order trade though. The first of these is the limit order, which sets a specific price at which the trade will be carried out. If that price never occurs, the trade is not executed. The investor is thus given the ability to specify the lowest price at which the stock will be sold or the highest price at which the stock will be bought. In essence, the limit order allows the investor to exert a degree of control over what price they find to be acceptable for their investment.

Another way around the conventional market order is the stop-market order. This is an order that tells the broker to execute the closing trade at a specific price. Stop-market orders are typically used as safeguards against catastrophic losses. For example, if a share of stock is purchased for $100, you might give your broker an order to sell the share if it drops below $90. This way, you have the opportunity to protect yourself from a devastating drop in the price of the stock.

Stop-limit orders combine limit orders and stop-market orders. With this type of trade, once the stop price is attained by the stock, the order simply becomes a limit order. Again, with this trading strategy, there is a risk that the trade will never be initiated if the stock never reaches the set price, and the trader who initiates such a trade will still be responsible for the brokerage fees associated with such a trade.

With the more advanced type of trades, the stockbroker demands a higher fee. Because of the nuances they entail, these trades are more difficult to carry out and require more attention to detail. However, they do provide a great service by guaranteeing that your trade will be executed at the prices you wish. Even if your trade is not executed and you are stuck with the fee, these trades are worth at least a glance; over the long run they will save you the headache of worrying that your order will be filled in time.

Although each online broker will be slightly different with the software they use, there are many similarities in how trades are conducted. To be an active trader, your most important tool is your computer. With a good computer and a high-speed Internet connection, you will have access to both your broker and your research tools. You will also need a software program that can make charts and graphs for you. While there are a few online chart construction tools, the majority of these do not show the most recent changes in price throughout the day. These charts are great for beginners, but if you wish to sell stocks short, you will need to-the-minute updates for the stocks you hold.

While Internet trading is the easiest and most expeditious way to trade, there is another option. If you do not feel comfortable with putting your information online, or you just want a more personal experience trading, there are still brokers out there that interact over the telephone. By talking to a live person, you are reducing your risk of processing errors or just plain oversights on your part. If you want to initiate a put option for 100 shares of J. Crew Group Inc. (JCG), you may accidentally mistake this for 100 contracts. This could be a costly error on your part since one option contract is for 100 shares. If you were to execute a put option of 100 contracts, you would be under contract for 10,000 shares of JCG. If you were speaking with a live broker, she would likely catch this mistake, saving you both money and stress.

Specializing

The art of specialization will not only save you time, it will increase the amount of money you make. Just as a professor of English literature will specialize in a specific time period or genre, you should consider specializing in a certain type of trading. There are a few things that you should take into account:

- **Type of analysis:** How best do you interpret data from stocks? Are you going to rely on technical or fundamental analysis? Technical analysis is reliant upon past and current prices and volume, and the many charts that can be made to measure both of these things. Fundamental analysis, on the other hand, takes a holistic look at a company, taking into account such factors as financial reports, earnings per share, and new innovations within a company.

- **Type of momentum:** Are you going to trade with current trends or bank on a trend coming to an end, hoping to find a top to a stock's price so that you can ride it on the way down with a short sell? There are two types of traders within this category: those who put their money into a stock that is already headed in a profitable direction, and those who put their money into a stock with the hopes that its price will reverse.

- **Type of system:** Will you be using concrete guidelines to dictate your trading, such as with a computer system, or will trades be left to your discretion allowing you a bit more wiggle room? Traders should plot out a trade prior to entering a position, regardless of what type of trade it is. This should include both an entry and an exit price. How strict their guidelines are is a point of contention amongst traders; should you use a computer system to plug in numbers and let the "system" determine entry and exit points? Or is it more profitable to use your individual discretion?

Just as the English professor may specialize in medieval literature but is aware of current trends in popular literature, traders must at least be knowledgeable of the other strategies out there, regardless of which specialization you choose. This will make you a better trader because you will be aware of more factors that play a part in determining the price of a stock. You should pick one but be able to double-check your strategy. This does not mean that you should change trade strategies back and forth during a trade. Pick a method that works and stick with it throughout the course of a trade. Once the trade is over, you can evaluate and adjust your strategy appropriately.

It should be noted that there is no right or wrong type of specialization. Neither side guarantees success, just as neither side will necessarily spell doom for traders. It is up to each individual to determine how they best make market decisions and how they best manage their portfolios. These are points that we will be returning to often throughout the book, hopefully making the identification of what works best for you a bit easier. There are a few other things that you will need to have mastery of before you start trading:

- Psychology: Do you understand both your own and other people's trading strategies?

- Money management: How do you best allocate your capital?

- Record keeping: How do you keep track of what trades you have made?

Trading psychology

Your trading psychology should take three things into consideration: your own personal psychology, how other people think, and how the market reacts to other people's actions. This is an expansive subject and many books have been written solely on this topic, however it can be broken down into one simple statement: do what works best for you. This involves both the amount of risk that you can consistently sustain and the amount that you want returned to you. By knowing yourself better, you will be less prone to making psychological mistakes. These include the fear and nervousness that occurs when you trade outside of your comfort zone.

If you know what works best for you, you will be touching upon all three considerations. You will also be more confident in your trading strategies because they will be tailored to your needs. The better you know yourself, the more adept you will be at navigating the stock market, and the more profits you will see. The better you know how other people will act in certain situations, the more talented you will be at finding trends that you may not have otherwise found. The better you know how the market will react to these past two points, the easier it will be for you to predict future actions within a stock's share price.

Selling stocks short can be an exhilarating process. Adrenaline junkies, gamblers, and thrill seekers can all get their kicks with short selling. However, this does not mean that they will profit when they make trades. You need to separate the euphoria of trading from the business aspect of it. Do you sell short because of the high you get? Or do you trade to make money? There is nothing wrong with feeling this euphoria, as long as you are honest with yourself about it. The moment you are entering trades just for that kick, you need to acknowledge that you will probably lose money.

Money management

Your money management techniques alone can ruin you. If you put all of your money into one poorly chosen stock, you will lose everything. Of course this is an extreme example, but the point is proven: Misallocation of your capital can spell certain disaster.

On the opposite side of the picture, good money management skills can help you to maximize your profits. By properly diversifying your portfolio you can minimize the effects of your bad stock choices and multiply the benefits of the good choices. No one will ever pick the right stocks 100 percent of the time, although this should not stop you from trying. This type of safety net is not only a good idea, it should be the centerpiece of your trading strategy. You will want to structure your trading so that your degree of risk is always minimized while your growth is maximized. Of course some trades are riskier than others, but there are always ways to reduce that degree of risk.

This can be accomplished in a number of ways. One of the best ways is to pick a certain percentage of your trading capital, usually 1–2 percent, and never put more at risk than that. By using a stop-loss point, you can invest more and risk less. How does this work? Assume you have $1,000 available to trade with and you feel comfortable risking 2 percent in a single trade. This means you cannot risk more than $20 per trade. If you were to enter a short sale of 10, $2 shares with only that $20, and the stock in question saw a 2 percent drop, you would earn a grand total of 40 cents. Even ignoring the fees that would be charged on this trade, this hardly seems like a worthwhile trade.

There is another option. In theory, you could place the entire $1,000 into the same trade. As long as you have a stop-loss price in place, this can be accomplished with only the same amount being placed at risk. Assume you are shorting 10 shares of a $100 stock. If the stock drops the same 2 percent, you would have a gain of $20. Even if you made a bad choice regarding the choice of stock to short, with a stop-loss point of $102, you would still only be down $20 (plus fees, of course). By risking the same $20, you are gaining $19.60. As you can see, by risking the same amount of money, you are earning much more. This type of trading is an extreme form and should only be conducted once you have gained quite a bit of confidence and experience with your short selling. Here are some other money management do's and do not's to be aware of:

- **Do not chase your losses:** You might think that you are bound to have a winning trade eventually, but the market probably will not agree with you. The more emotionally involved you become with your trades, the less likely they are to be profitable.

- **Do pick a number you can stand to lose during a given month:** This number can be either a percentage of capital or a dollar amount. Once you lose that amount, stop trading for the rest of the month. Take the time to sit back and learn from your mistakes.

- **Do not subscribe to a set system:** One famous system used by gamblers is the Martingale system, which works by doubling the amount of trade after each losing trade. For example, the first trade would be $1, the second $2, the third $4, the fourth $8, and so on. This is a sure-fire route to ruin. While in theory this will produce small gains, it does not take into account that oftentimes you will lose many trades in a row. It also is not conducive to people trading large amounts of money. The Martingale system only works if you are successful within your first few trades. As you will undoubtedly see both in your own trading and within the case studies in this book it is common to have several failed trades in a row. Losses add up very quickly with this system if you do not have an infinite amount of money to trade with.

- **Do handle each trade separately:** When you are calculating the amount of risk you are willing to take on, it is important that each trade stands alone — even if you have multiple trades with the same company at the same time. This will make your record keeping much simpler.

- **Do take slippage into account:** There are many fees associated with trading. This is especially true with short selling. If you trade without considering these fees, you might have several successful trades, yet still be unprofitable. You need to trade amounts large enough to overcome slippage, yet not so much that you are uncomfortable.

Risk control

Risk control is also a large part of money management but warrants a separate look. The amount of risk that you can handle will determine the amount of shares you end up selling short. This can be quantified with a gain-to-loss ratio. As a general rule, you should avoid trades that have a gain-to-loss ratio of less than 2:1. Ignoring margin leverage, assume you begin trading with $100,000, and you are looking at a short sale of 10 shares of Apple Inc. (AAPL) stock, which happens to be right at $200 per share in this hypothetical situation. If you are willing to stick with the trade until shares rise to $204, a 2 percent rise, then you need to plan accordingly because by taking this trade, you are putting only $40 at risk ($4 x 10 shares = $40). The amount being risked is only $40 because you have placed a stop-loss point so that you cannot lose more than this amount.

If you are going to trade with 2 percent of your available capital, you will be shorting 10 shares for $2,000 worth of Apple's stock. You fully expect Apple's stock to drop 5 percent down to $190 and can justifiably set this as your profit target, which will give you a 5 percent gain based on the amount that you have placed in this trade, or $100. This gives you a gain-to-loss ratio of 5:2, (100:40 simplifies to 5:2.) This is just slightly higher than our threshold of 2:1 and can therefore be viewed as a worthwhile trade.

Having the appropriate stops is another necessity. This might mean paying for a stop-loss point. Your other option, if you plan on day trading, is to set a theoretical stop-loss point and cover your position manually if and when the stock rises to that point. This is not something suggested for newer traders because it takes quite a bit of discipline to actually carry out. The automatic stop-loss point is much more suitable if you are new or not planning on day trading.

Record keeping

You can learn from both your positive and your negative trades. Sometimes it is the losing trades that you will learn the most from. Either way, as a successful trader, you will be making hundreds of trades, so how can you expect to remember the details from them all? Although there may be some gifted individuals out there with expansive memories, the majority of us are not so lucky. By recording each and every trade, you will find patterns in your trading, both positive and negative. True, your first trade may have been successful, but if you do not develop a pattern of successful trades afterwards, you will soon be facing financial ruin.

If you do not learn from the past mistakes you have made, you will never grow as a trader. By keeping a detailed record of your trades, including your thought process leading up to entering the position, you will begin to see what makes a successful trade and what makes a terrible one. Many brokers allow you to take screen snapshots of the pricing charts you look at and incorporate it into an online diary. This is a very beneficial tool. More importantly, though, a good record keeping system spills over into all aspects of your trading regimen. You will be able to gauge where your strengths and weaknesses are as a trader, and it will force you to hold yourself accountable for your actions. It will also help you specialize your trading, which, as you will see, can help multiply your profits.

A spreadsheet program is also a valuable tool. With a Microsoft® Excel spreadsheet, you can document the company, the number of shares shorted, the amount of money traded, the length of time before the trade was closed, and the amount gained or lost all in one place. With the tabs option, you can even sort trades by the week or month they take place in. Extra time should be taken to study past trades. There will always be profitable trades out there, but you will not be able to spot them if you are not taking away the knowledge and feedback that the market provides. A record of losing trades is better than a string of unrecorded profits because of this. A year after those winning trades, how will you remember them and learn from them if they are not fully documented?

On top of a visual record, you should grade your performance. Assign a letter grade to each trade three times; once for the entry, once for the exit, and once for the overall trade. There are two parts to each trade, and you can learn from each separately. On top of this, you should be evaluating the trade in its entirety so that you can see all of the elements of both successes and failures. These grades cannot be assigned, obviously, until after the trade has concluded and you have seen how the stock in question performed after you have ended your position. If you enter a position and the stock climbs even higher before dropping down, you would then not give yourself as high of a grade as you would if the entry to the trade was at the stock's peak price.

The amount of money made or lost should not be the defining factor in your grading. Anyone can get lucky on an ill-advised trade and make a lot of money on a one-time basis. Does this make it a better trade than the beginner who plots out their ideal trade, waits a month for the sell signal to occur, shorts the stock, and makes a very small profit before exiting the trade? Of course not. The latter trade is by far a smarter trade. Just because it did not net as much of a profit does not mean that it was a weaker trade. When you grade your trades, you should be doing so based on a few factors:

- How close was the trade's entry point to the relative high point in the stock's price?

- How close was the trade's exit point to the relative low point in the stock's price?

- How long did it take for the trade to reach the exit point?

These three questions should guide you when assigning a grade to each and every one of your trades. If you want to assign a more accurate grade to your trades, consider a number grade. The easi-

est way to assign a number grade to your entry and exit points is by determining the percentage of the short-term high or low, respectively, that your trade was at. A week prior to the trade, the time during which the trade was open, and a week after the trade should be looked at when determining number grades. For example, assume you initiate a short sale of IBM at $98. A couple days after the trade concludes, the stock rises to $100. This trade would then have scored a 98 overall on its entry point.

Each and every trade will not be a winning one, but if you keep a trade diary, you can become a better trader with each transac-tion, regardless of whether it makes money. This strategy is als a great way for monitoring slippage. If you find that you are su cessful but still losing money because of fees and commissio you can either adjust by trading with more money or switch cheaper, yet similar, broker.

A Word Regarding Taxes

The taxation of investments is a complicated process. Wh capital gains tax currently sits at 15 percent, come 2011, th rate is set to revert back to the previous rate of 20 percen ever, there are still many ways to reduce your tax burde a complete look at the capital gains tax is outside the real book, some of the more common questions and concern ing the taxation of your trades, along with a few ways you can reduce your tax burden.

For starters, only *realized* gains and losses need to be your tax return paperwork. This means that only th you have covered during a particular tax year must

The trades that are left open do not need to be reported. For both long and short selling traders, this will be all, or at least the vast majority of your trades because of the short lifespan that your trades will have before you buy back your positions. Remember: You are not going to be holding short positions for very long.

Deferring losses

According to current tax laws, you can report your losing trades as well as your winning ones when it comes time to file your taxes. One of the more common ways of reducing your tax burden is by carrying forward your losses. This can be done on an indefinite basis and can offset your capital gains taxes to an extent. Also called tax gain/loss harvesting, this process allows traders to defer the reporting of losses for as long as they feel it necessary. Currently, you can use up to $3,000 each year to help offset your capital gains taxes. Therefore, if you lose more than $3,000 during the course of a year, you can carry that loss to the next year. For example, assume you conducted a trade that lost $10,000. At the end of the year, you can only use $3,000 as a loss on your tax forms, leaving $7,000 in losses that were not accounted for. You can use $3,000 of that loss in your next year's tax documents, allowing you to maximize the tax break that you will receive the following year.

Many traders know this, yet a surprisingly small number of them actually do this. For some, it is the difficulty in admitting defeat. For most others, it is simply poor record keeping. If you do not keep track of all your trades, especially your losses, you will not have an idea of what kind of taxes you should be paying. Because you can use losses to offset gains, it is extremely important that

you have a firm grasp on what each trade has done for your over-all bankroll.

There are a few exceptions to the tax gain/loss harvesting rule, the most prevalent being the "wash-sale" rule. This law prohibits the use of a loss as a tax write off if the same stock is repurchased within 30 days of the original loss. So if you sell short 100 shares of Ford (F) at $10, and the stock rise to $13, you will have a $300 loss. Now that the stock is at a new relative high, you might be thinking that there is no way it can sustain that high. As true as that may be, you cannot enter another trade with the same com-pany until 30 days have elapsed if you want to use the $300 loss to offset short-term capital gains.

False withholdings

So you have begun short selling, only to discover that you are extremely good at it. In fact, you have made $10,000 in winning trades over the course of your first calendar year and only $3,000 in losing ones. Remember tax loss harvesting? You can use that $3,000 to offset some of your earnings. Now, it looks like you will have $7,000 in taxable earnings according to short-term capital gains laws. 15 percent of $7,000 is $1,050 that you now owe to the IRS.

$1,050 is a decently sized chunk of money, but even if it was only a few dollars, not paying it to the IRS is considered to be tax eva-sion. There is a vast difference between tax reduction and tax eva-sion. According to the IRS, each individual has the right to reduce his or her tax burden; in other words, each tax payer has the right to take advantage of any tax credits, reductions, or write-offs that will apply to their situation and effectively lower how much they owe Uncle Sam. Tax breaks and write-offs are legal; not reporting all of your income in an effort to avoid paying taxes, on the other hand, is considered a criminal act.

The legal rights of short sellers

When a broker falsely advertises a financial product, either by manipulating past performance data or with guarantees of a future performance, investors oftentimes have the right to sue the brokerage for misleading them. However, short sellers, because they are not outright owners of the shares of stock they trade, do not have this luxury. So if a law suit were to emerge regarding a brokerage's fraudulent claims, any short sellers that worked with that broker would not be able to become part of that lawsuit.

In the past, companies have been able to sue short sellers for defamation, though. This does not happen because of short selling, but rather it happens because of a short seller's doings. By making claims that a company is doing poorly, when in fact it is not, it may encourage people to abandon their long positions, thus lowering the actual price of that company's stock. It is best to avoid making derogatory comments regarding a company, especially on an online forum or blog where there are many visitors. This can be construed as a way to artificially drive down stock prices and may make you susceptible to a lawsuit.

Market Overview Conclusion

There are few things about the stock market that are proven. Market conditions are fluid and dynamic; the market is always changing, always adjusting to reflect a business's growth and consumer sentiment. Because of this, you will never fully understand the market. This should not alarm you: it is half the fun of playing the market — the other half is making money, of course.

One thing to keep in mind is that it is a proven fact that markets oscillate. Overall market conditions go up and down with the stocks that comprise them. While the market does have an over-all upward trend, this does not hold true for individual stocks. Companies decline in price all the time, but few people take advantage of both sides of the market, choosing to maximize their profits during upswings and minimize downswings. You are not like these other people; otherwise you would not have picked up this book. The next chapter introduces a vast concept that will allow you to profit when stocks take a turn for the worst: short selling.

Oscillation is Your Friend

The term oscillation refers to the fact that stocks do not move in straight lines. There are constant ups and downs, both over the long- and short-term. The market flows quite like a wave in the ocean as prices rise and fall. In fact, regardless of the time period of a stock's price chart, you will see these oscillations. Day traders use daily oscillations to make quick profits while position traders will wait for weeks sometimes for an oscillation cycle to run its course. Do not be intimidated by the fluidity of the stock market. Just like a wave in the ocean, what comes up will go down.

Chapter 2

An Introduction to Selling Stocks Short

Contrary to the traditional method of trading, selling a stock short is done with the hope that the price of the stock will drop. Most people have little clue as to the mechanics of how this works. The process of short selling is misunderstood for several reasons. It is, in fact, a complicated and intricate method of trading, but because of the taboo surrounding shorting, it only appears to be more difficult to understand than it actually is. Short selling is also counterintuitive. How does one manage to profit from the declining price of a stock? Is it even ethical to profit when all those around you are losing their money?

Shorting is controversial. Short sellers have been blamed on several occasions for systemic market collapses, such as the Great Depression of the 1930s. There have been alleged ties between espionage and profiting from the demise of American stock markets. There was even an investigation after Sept. 11 to see if Osama bin Laden had shorted airline and insurance stocks. There was no evidence found to support this claim, but it does show the paranoia and fear that the public has concerning shorting the stock market. During both peaceful times and times of distress there have been allegations of fraud in regards to short sellers.

Short sellers are often accused of fraud and greed, but these things can occur within any section of the market; one only needs to look as far as the headlines of recent newspapers to see this. Consider the Enron scandal, Bernard Madoff's Ponzi scheme, or the inflated bonuses paid to bank officers after their companies were given government money through TARP to keep them from going belly up. None of these involved short selling, yet they were some of the single most detrimental events in the economy's recent woes. Still, short sellers have developed a bad reputation over the years.

In reality, shorting the stock market is a vital part of keeping markets balanced and regulated. In an overbought market, short sellers bring prices down safely and efficiently, making crashes less severe. Shorting is a valuable tool that keeps individual stocks within a realistic price range; overvaluation is avoided this way. In fact, short selling helps to stabilize otherwise turbulent markets. The market has two sides, a bull and a bear, an up and a down. Short sellers comprise the down side, which as any stock chart will tell you, is just as natural and necessary as the up.

The short selling process varies drastically from taking a long position in the market, and because few people understand it, the shorting process is clouded in mystique. Instead of buying a stock through a stock broker and hoping the particular stock bought will increase in price, the short trader is borrowing the stock from a stock broker and immediately selling it, hoping that it will go down in price, so that when the price declines, the short trader will be able to then buy the shares at the lower price and return them to the broker and pocket the difference. Although short selling comes with dangers, it is not something that should be avoided. True, there is the risk that a stock might rise in price and cause the trader to lose money, but there is an element of risk that comes with any variable investment. If you use safeguards, this risk is minimized. The infinite risk that so many traders shun is something you will never have to worry about if you trade correctly.

An Inexact Science

With all the dangers of short selling, why would anyone choose to partake in it? There are several answers to this question, but perhaps the most enticing answer is the security it brings. This might sound contradictory at first. How can such a dangerous activity, one that even has an infinite amount of risk, bring about financial security?

Surprisingly, short selling can be an important part of a well-balanced portfolio. The main idea behind diversification is that if your investments are truly spread out, you are protecting yourself if any one of them fails by counting on the other investments' gains to minimize the loss. This is why hedge funds have become so popular. Hedge funds, a basket fund that attempts to make up for losses in other portfolio areas, have appeal because oftentimes they will perform well in poor markets, or at least perform better than traditional funds. In essence, what a hedge fund does is attempt to provide gains when the overall market is in a downturn. This is often accomplished through short selling.

Why Does Selling Short Work?

If the stock you borrow changes price, why does the broker allow people to sell the stock short? One share of a company's stock is legally the same as one share of stock, regardless of any change in price; the percentage of ownership that the individual the stock is borrowed from does not change with price. Therefore, there is no difference to the brokers who let you borrow the stock, even if the price has changed. Brokers will make money regardless of how the stock performs. When you borrow a share of stock from a broker, they are letting you borrow something that does not change, regardless of what happens to its price. The degree of partial ownership is maintained as long as the same number of shares is returned, despite any discrepancies in the stock's costs between when you borrow them and when you return them.

Another major reason why selling short is a worthwhile task is because of the way in which markets have acted over the course of history. It is an established fact that stocks fall in price quicker than they rise. This allows you to accomplish two valuable things with your money: keeping your money in high-risk transactions for shorter periods of time and conducting more money-making transactions than you would if you held long positions for the same amount of time.

Short selling, and trading in general, is not for those who want an exact answer. If you want a guarantee, put your money into a cash savings account or a fixed annuity. Instead, short sellers must look at many different factors and extrapolate their conclusion from those seemingly abstract clues. *There will be hints and warning signs along the way to forming a decision, which will be* discussed in Chapters 11–12. But even knowing the warning signs, the best short seller still gets it wrong sometimes. When looking at a company, there should be some sort of warning or danger sign that stands out, separating that company from the rest. Perhaps the earnings statements that a corporation has just posted were well below their sector's average. Perhaps their accounting system has allegations of fraud surrounding it. There needs to be some sort of trigger that lets the trader know that the stock is ready to be sold short.

Risks of Selling Short

There are a few major risks associated with selling short. Although these risks are very real, they are also very avoidable.

Inflation

If you invest your money for a long period of time, inflation becomes a major factor with your investment. If your investment does not keep up with inflation, you are basically losing money. Since the Great Depression, the market has gained on average 3 percent per year. Short selling, however, does not keep up with inflation since the overall direction of the market is upward and short sales rely on a decline in price. This makes short selling only suitable for very short-termed trades. If you are making a long-term investment, short selling is not a suitable strategy.

Infinite losses

Technically, there is infinite risk involved with selling a stock short. If you borrow 100 shares of Boeing Company's (BA) stock at $50 expecting it to fall to $40, you will be netting a $1,000 gain because 100 shares multiplied by a $10 change equals $1,000 — minus any fees or interest that the broker may charge, of course. But suppose that the stock rises to $100 per share before you cover your position: That is a $5,000 loss you will have to make up for when selling the stock back to the broker. What if the stock's price rises to $250? That is $20,000 down the drain. Now, you are facing substantial, and possibly life-changing, losses.

There is no limit to how high a stock's price might rise, but a stock can only fall to zero — there are no negative share prices. Is it realistic that a stock's price will jump this high with no warning? Probably not. Besides, before you enter any trade you should have an emergency exit strategy, preferably an automatic one. **Stop-loss points**, an order to your broker to cancel your position when the price reaches a certain point, can be built into any trade, assuming that your broker allows these. Although there may be an additional fee for a stop-loss price to be set, it is well worth it if it prevents a catastrophic loss such as with the above example.

Dividends

If a company declares dividends during the period in which you have an open short sale, the person or entity that owns the shares is still entitled to that money. Where does this money come from if they technically do not have the shares any longer?

You may have guessed this already, but the dividend proceeds comes from the short sellers own coffers. That is right: You are responsible for supplying the broker with the dividend proceeds for the shares you have borrowed. For example, assume that you borrow 100 share of Apple Inc. (AAPL), and it announces dividend earnings at $0.05 per share. You will be entitled to repay that $5 to broker, so that they may pay the person whose shares you have borrowed. If the dividends were reported at $10 per share, you would then have to repay $1,000. Known as the ex-dividend date, brokers will set a date that the dividend proceeds must be collected by. When the ex-dividend date passes, the amount due is subtracted from the short seller's margin account and given to the original owner of the stock.

This risk is a bit more difficult to avoid. Some companies are serial dividend providers where once a quarter or once a year, they will supply a certain amount per share to its shareholders in the form of dividends. The timing of dividends is usually consistent from payment to payment, usually occurring shortly after the quarterly earnings meetings. By being aware of a company's inner workings and fundamental traits, you can time your short sales around these occurrences. Looking over earnings reports when they are released as well as analysts' opinions on different companies will alert you to the vast majority of dividend releases. You should then be able to avoid the bulk of dividend disbursements.

Buy in

A **buy in** occurs when a broker demands that your position be covered immediately. This mostly happens after a stock that you have shorted rises drastically in price. Brokers are able to do this because of the margin account contract that you sign when setting up your account. The contract will state that the broker can recall borrowed stocks on a moment's notice. The broker does not necessarily need to have a reason. This is not done with malicious intent — you are after all only paying interest on these borrowed shares — and the broker may need to have them returned out of necessity. If the stock is quickly rising in price or if the original owner sells their shares for some reason, a buy in is definitely needed in order for the broker to save face and live up to its obligations to his other clients.

Short squeeze

A **short squeeze** occurs when there is a panic amongst short sellers, and they attempt to buy back the shares they originally sold. As you know, when there is an increase in demand for a product, prices will rise in order to bring in the most revenue for the amount of demand. In this case, the price of each share will increase, causing things to quickly spin out of control with the artificial increase in demand. Suppose you have borrowed 100 shares of International Business Machines Corp. (IBM) and sold them short for $100 per share. But rather than going down as you had hoped, IBM's stock keeps increasing, and soon it is at $125 per share. But this is not where it ends. Because other short sellers have met their stop-loss points, they are buying back shares in order to cover their positions. This creates a higher demand for the shares, causing the price to increase. Others who have sold IBM shares short are now met with an increasing price, and as they cover that price by repurchasing the stock, the stock's price keeps increasing. By the time you finally are able to cover your position, the stock is up to $150 per share, and you net a $5,000 loss, plus the ever-present brokerage fees and commission.

The short squeeze is usually not found in stocks that have high prices as the example above does, but this does not make them any less dangerous. There is a simple way to avoid short squeezes though. The phenomenon described above can only take place if the stock meets two conditions: the company's volume is very low, and there is a high percentage of short sellers with open positions in the particular company. A stock's volume is the number of shares traded per day. If this number is low, price manipulations can occur with greater ease, giving rise to the dangers of a short squeeze.

Free riding

Because many short sellers are day and swing traders, free riding can become a serious problem for them. **Free riding** is the term for selling off a stock before the purchase of it has settled. In general, a trade takes three days to finalize. Short sellers often will sell and then buy back stocks in a period of time shorter than those three days using leveraged margin accounts. When the trade is conducted with insufficient funds, a problem arises. If there has been no prior credit arrangement made with the broker, your account will be frozen for 90 days, and you will be required to pay the amount owed instantly. This, of course, can be avoided if you have sufficient funds within your cash account.

Margin Accounts

A margin account is an account comprised of cash and stock shares that can be borrowed by the broker you are working with and lent to other traders. It also happens to be one of the greatest dangers that a new short seller may face; yet brokerages require the short seller to own a margin account in order to trade. Because the trader must borrow the shares he wishes to sell, there is no actual monetary exchange at first. Instead, the broker gives the short trader shares of the stock from other traders' margin accounts. A mandatory agreement made prior to opening any margin account is that the broker is allowed to borrow shares from other clients' margin accounts at any given time. This is a blessing for short sellers. It allows a larger number of shares to be borrowed by other short sellers. If there are no shares available from other clients' accounts or partner brokerages, the trade will not be able to take place.

A margin account can be a dangerous tool if not used with caution. While it is a requirement in order to sell short thanks to Regulation T, margin accounts can cause financial ruin if not properly run. As opposed to a cash account, where cash is evenly exchanged for the stock purchased, a margin account is in essence an account that allows you to borrow stock with cash and other stocks used as collateral. When you borrow from your broker, you will be charged interest as with any other type of loan. The interest rate is relatively low when compared to other loans, such as credit cards, but it is still a relevant factor that must be understood and accounted for by the trader when using margin.

Regulation T

The Federal Reserve's Regulation T dictates the amount of money that can be leveraged within a margin account. Currently, this regulation states that for every $1 in a margin account, $2 worth of stock can be traded. Traders using margin are subject to the approval of the broker they wish to go through and may have credit checks run with their social security number to see if they are a credit risk to the brokerage. Borrowed money is also subject to an interest rate determined by the brokerage.

Brokers will allow you to borrow stocks if you have at least 50 percent of the value of the marginable stocks in your account. Marginable products include most bonds, stocks currently valued at over $3 in the New York Stock Exchange, stocks currently valued at over $4 in the NASDAQ, and most mutual funds, as long as they are held for at least a month. For example, if you have $5,000 worth of marginable stock in your account, your borrowing power would then be $10,000. When that value goes up, your borrowing power and your leverage will also go up.

However, brokers have a tool to protect themselves from overly enthusiastic borrowing. The margin call is a tool that the broker will use if they feel that the short seller has taken too dangerous of a position. This may also be referred to as a maintenance call. This might take the shape of a well-established blue-chip stock that is quickly rising in price or a volatile stock that has seen many severe ups and downs. Since the short seller does not flat out own the stocks they are trading, the broker is able to demand that the position be settled at any given moment. In essence, the broker would void the loan and the stocks would need to be returned or the current market price of the borrowed stocks plus interest be repaid. Margin calls can spell ruin if you cannot cover your position. The broker does not need to give the trader any forewarning regarding margin calls and is legally able to sell off your other securities within the margin account in order to meet their demands. However, most brokers, depending on the situation, will give some sort of warning prior to taking such drastic steps. If you are the one to initiate contact with the broker, sometimes they will even work out a repayment plan with you.

Because margined dollars are essentially borrowed from a broker, the broker will apply an interest rate when you use your margin account. This interest rate would be applied to the value of the shares borrowed from the broker. Margin accounts can be visualized as a sort of safety net for the broker. They allow the brokerage to get the money back that was borrowed from them at any time they wish. On the other hand, they also allow the trader to use money that they do not necessarily have in order to make a profit. This mixed blessing must be treated with caution, but it can lead to great results if properly used. The risk of a margin call can never be avoided completely, but you can do your best by being judicious when it comes to the selection of which stocks you are shorting. The best way to avoid a margin call is by picking the right stocks.

Reserves and Preservation of Capital

The more money you put into a trade, the higher risk the trade is. This may sound like common sense, but it is something that eludes many traders. You never want to put a large percentage of your trading capital into a single trade, no matter how "sure" of a profit there might be.

When beginning selling short, you will want to play with small numbers. If you are beginning with $5,000, perhaps 1 percent, or $50, of that should go into a single trade. This might seem like it is not even worth the trouble, and that is entirely the point. The less risk you face, the less amount of money at stake, the more sensible you will act regarding the trade. With small amounts of money, your emotions will not play as large of a part in your trade execution. Once you are able to calmly establish trades, you may start increasing the percentage of money you put into the market. As your bankroll increases in size, you can systematically begin increasing the amount you are trading. For example, 1 percent of $5,000 is only $50, but if you have increased your bankroll to $10,000, while keeping the percentage the same at 1 percent, you can now trade with $100 on a single trade.

The phenomenon that poker players call "tilt" is a major factor for long- and short-term traders alike. Tilt is a poker term that means you are letting your emotions become a part of your play. It is a sure-fire way to lose money, in poker and in the stock market. When you make a trade that is beyond your comfort zone, you might feel nervous or giddy. You might even be exhilarated. The worst thing that can happen here is a successful trade. Why? Because a successful trade will only encourage you to act in the same manner again or perhaps make an even bigger trade. Sooner or later, you are bound to make a mistake. When this happens, your bankroll will be devastated. But if the point of putting your money in the stock market is to make money, why would you want to trade with such small amounts? There are a few reasons:

- You are just beginning to learn about an impossibly huge subject. Because it is such a huge undertaking, you are going to be prone to mistakes, especially in the beginning. Besides, no one will ever master the stock market; there are just too many variables to take into account.

- You want to preserve your capital for when you are more experienced, more confident, and more humble. Do not waste your money when you are still in the beginning stages and more likely to make a mistake.

- You will want reserves for when a good trade becomes even better.

Cash reserves

Sometimes, a good trade will become a great trade, although the process for this might seem counterintuitive. For example, you short 10 shares of IBM stock for $100 per share. Every indicator is saying that the stock will drop to $75, maybe even more. But a week later, the stock stays near the top of the chart, even going up to $105. As long as this is not at or above your stop-loss point, there is no reason to panic. In fact, your indicators have not changed; you are still convinced that the stock is going to drop fast and hard. If the $1,000 you fronted for the trade was all the trading capital you had, you would be in a very tight spot. However, you are a savvy trader — you only put 1 percent of your available capital into the trade. This gives you a large cash reserve to draw from and make even more money.

Instead of panicking, you short another 10 shares of IBM, this time for $1,050, or $105 per share. Another week goes by, and finally the stock begins to drop, just like you expected. Rather than locking up all of your money and facing a potential loss or margin call, you had a cash reserve that allowed you to reinforce your trade and more than double the amount of money you would have made otherwise. A reserve of cash is also a good idea in case a margin call occurs. Rather than scrambling to find the money, you would have it readily available for your broker. When IBM hits $75 per share, you cover your position and profit $550, minus fees and commission. If the $1,000 was all of your trading capital, you may have faced a margin call from your nervous broker when the stock rose in price. At the very best, you would have made only $250, minus the fees and commission.

Which of these hypothetical trades looks more attractive to you?

Short interest

Short interest refers to the percentage of shares within a company that are currently shorted versus the total amount of shares that can be shorted. The latter number is determined by taking the total number of outstanding shares that have been shorted but not covered and dividing that number by the **free float**, which is determined by taking all of the outstanding shares of a stock and subtracting from it the number of stocks that cannot be sold short. This includes shares held by officers and executives, strategic shareholders, and insiders' stock holdings. All of this information is sent from the broker to the stock exchanges where these numbers are posted for the public to view.

The short interest ratio will rarely be more than 15 percent. Most often, this number will be below 10 percent, meaning that less than 10 percent of the entire company's shares are in the midst of being shorted. The higher the short interest ratio is, the more bearish people have become regarding the stock. This is good for short sellers, but only up to a point. The more people who have shorted a particular stock, the more likely that a short squeeze will occur. If some event takes place that necessitates a selling off of the stock, you may get burned as stock prices rise when more and more people buy back shares to cover their positions.

Days to cover

The days to cover indicator is another way of telling us how crowded the market is in respect to short sellers. If you are concerned because of a high short interest ratio, the days to cover statistic may resolve the issue for you. Days to cover is calculated by dividing the stock's short interest ratio number by the total daily volume. This measurement will tell you how many days it would take if all short sellers panicked at the same time and covered their positions:

$$\frac{\text{Amount of shares sold short}}{\text{Average daily volume}}$$

This calculation is sometimes also called a stock's short interest ratio. Indeed, for all of the short sellers of a particular stock to panic and cover their positions would be an extremely rare occurrence, but it is always a possibility. Ideally, this number should be less than 1, indicating that the stock is very safe. A high short interest ratio can be neutralized if the stock trades at a high enough volume. If the days to cover number rises to more than 20 though, the stock is considered to be very dangerous to invest because there are far too many short sellers involved. In this case, a short squeeze is extremely likely.

What it Takes to be Successful

Short selling is not an easy way to make money. It requires nerves of steel and a strong stomach for weathering losses. Still, with a good amount of determination and hard work, almost anyone can be successful in this style of trading. You can make trading a full-time job if you have the patience, knowledge, and drive to keep learning and expanding your skills. You will also need to be relentless because not every trade will be a successful one. A strong will to succeed will help you smooth over those losses. There might be times when you experience a margin call or your stop-loss price is hit before any money can be made. These are all natural parts of the learning experience and will happen to even the best short sellers. Do not worry: With practice, you will not only learn from these occurrences, you will learn to profit from them.

Just because a trade hits a stop-loss point does not mean that the trade is over. Continue to watch these trades, and be ready to jump back into them if an attractive price is hit. If the stock is continuously in a state that meets your short selling criteria, there is nothing wrong with reexamining the trade and even setting up a new one.

Chapter 3

What You Need to Begin

B efore you begin trading, there are several things you will need. Think of trading in general and short selling in particular as your own start-up business. There is always going to be an overhead cost before you can open up shop and start making money. Once you make it through the opening process of investing in yourself, you will be ready to invest in the market and start reaping the rewards of selling short. There is a rather lengthy learning curve associated with trading, especially short-term trading; you cannot expect to master it in a week, or even a year. Trading is a craft as well. Not only is there an investment of money, you must also invest time in learning the market and learning the timing of short sales. Patience is necessary at this stage. This is not only a knowledge factor; it is a matter of confidence. As a new short seller, the more you know about the market and how it acts, the better prepared you will be to handle the ups and downs that are inevitable. Still, nothing beats experience. Although this book serves as a great starting point, there is no replacement for time spent watching and observing the market.

Select a Broker and Trading Platform

There are dozens of reputable brokerage firms out there, all eagerly awaiting your commission. Selecting one is sometimes a daunting task, but if you know what you are looking for, you have nothing to fear.

Make a checklist of what you require from a broker and then shop around. Do not be afraid to look at several different brokers, this is the only way you will be able to see which one best suits your needs. Sometimes, you can only view fee and commission schedules if you are a member of the site. This does not mean that you will have to deposit money into an account with the particular site; merely give some personal information such as name, contact information, and trading experience and you will be able to register with the firm to see what it has to offer.

Finding the Right Online Broker

Once you determine which online stockbroker works best to fit your needs as a trader, there are some things that you should be aware of. As per law, you must supply your broker with personal information, including your social security number. This is not meant as an invasion of your privacy; it is one of the many safeguards the government has created in order to track both application of taxes and combat the criminal act of money laundering.

Constructing a pros and cons list may help if you are stuck deciding between two or three different brokers. If you are looking for a broker that has cheap fees for traditional short sales, do you consider a higher put option charge a fair trade? Only you can make this decision for yourself. Writing down your thought process might point out something that was otherwise not obvious at first glance. Your trading platform is equally important. There is no point in using brokers if the tools they supply are not adequate for your needs. You will want to make sure that your broker allows you to contain all of the features that you wish to use. Some of these include:

- Use of a margin account.
- Selling stocks short.
- Selling put options.
- Access to the forex market.
- Allowing commodity futures trading.
- Analyst opinions regarding stock choices.
- Real-time price charts.
- Access to market news.
- Portfolio management tools.
- Different types of orders.

Technology

As mentioned in Chapter 1, the first thing you will need in order to begin short selling is a computer and a high-speed Internet connection. Short sellers especially need to have real-time updates on stock prices because stock prices can and do change dramatically in just a few minutes, and if you are not aware of the changes immediately, it could cost you thousands of dollars. You will also need the most reliable stock charting software you can find. You may have to purchase this online, or your broker may supply a package for you when you sign up with them. Either way, the ability to create your own charts is imperative. This will allow you to mold your trading strategy to best fit your needs.

Ease of use and which indicators are provided are certainly important factors to weigh when deciding which brokerage to choose. If all else fails, you can sign up with a few different brokers, test their software out with paper trading, and see which one best suits what you are looking for. Because charting is such a vital aspect of determining when to enter and exit a position, you should not settle for mediocre packages. Think of this as another investment; you have to spend money to make money, and the better your charting package, the better your chances of making money. You will definitely need a software package that allows you to do more than just look at price charts. Something that allows you to track your trade dollars, account statistics, and your thoughts regarding each trade is going to be much more suitable to your needs than a free site. Of course, you can always keep a separate journal and track these things on your own, but a software package will save you time and energy. The software and analysis packages found on Dr. Alexander Elder's Web site, **www.elder. com**, are very versatile, and they are geared toward tracking your trades and saving you time during your trading day.

When it comes to technology, some traders will even use multiple computer screens in order to streamline their trading. With all of the different things your computer can do for you, this makes sense. How else can you efficiently show price charts, conduct research into a company's financial reports, and show the daily movement of several different stocks all at the same time? A second or even a third screen gives you more room to carry out all of your necessary tasks when it comes to trading.

When looking at past data, there are several good charting Web sites out there that do not charge a usage fee. These include, but are certainly not limited to:

- **BigCharts (www.bigcharts.marketwatch.com):** BigCharts hosts a wide array of different charting options. You have the ability to choose your type of chart, including candlestick charts. There is generally a delay in how often updates are made, so this is not the best option for day traders.

- **Yahoo! Finance (http://finance.yahoo.com):** Yahoo! contains many different charting options. While this site does have real-time updates, the charts are not as accommodating as other sites.

- **StockCharts (www.stockcharts.com):** StockCharts hosts perhaps the most comprehensive selection of options when it comes to creating charts. With the wide selection comes more complexity, though. If you are looking for simple, easy to use charts, this is not the site for you.

Paper Trading

Once you have your broker and chart-making program selected, you will need some practice. Known as paper trading, most brokers will let you buy and sell stocks with make believe money. It is much better to work out the rookie kinks with fake money than it is to lose real money. Because we are dealing with short selling, the potential for losses is infinite. In order to prevent that, practice is necessary.

This is not to say that once you begin trading real money nothing will ever be lost. There will always be losses. But the more experienced you are, the better prepared you will be to minimize these losses. Still, the best way to learn is by doing, especially when it comes to the stock market. Make sure that your broker's practice site allows you to sell stocks short since there are some brokers out there that do not allow short sales with their paper trading programs. Thinkorswim is one of the more popular sites when it comes to paper trading. Other Web sites, such as **www.cnbc.com**, sometimes have paper trading contests with cash prizes.

It should also be noted that paper trading will not mimic the emotions that real trading provokes. Just as if you were not playing poker for money, you will not feel attached to the paper trades as you would if you would with the money used when actual trading takes place. Because of this, you should always begin trading with very small amounts of money; about 1–2 percent of your bankroll is more than enough to begin with.

Bankroll

Most importantly, you will need a **bankroll**, a sum of money that is set aside exclusively for trading. Many experts contend that you should not start short selling with less than $10,000. This may seem like a large number to start with, but if you are not disciplined with your money management, it will disappear quickly. In reality, you can begin short selling with much less if you do have the discipline to manage it properly. Still, $10,000 is commonly the industry standard for beginning traders because the cost associated with short selling is so high, and it is a number large enough to give you some wiggle room with the fees and commissions your broker will charge you and will easily let you invest enough with each individual trade to overcome these obstacles. Another reason why $10,000 is an agreed upon amount is because of the fact that the learning curve is so steep for beginners. This "tuition" for learning how to judge the market can be partially avoided by beginning your trading with small amounts of money after you feel completely comfortable with paper trading.

Over the short-term, it will be hard to make a profit with short selling if you are not trading with large amounts, but this does not mean it is impossible to profit with smaller amounts; it just is more difficult. Some sites, such as **www.thinkorswim.com**, will not even let you begin trading with a margin account until you have at least $3,500 within the account. This is definitely a consideration that should be taken into account when selecting your broker. Although this may seem like a large amount, they must require such a high amount of collateral in order to protect themselves from the plagues of overeager and undereducated traders and investors.

In reality, you can begin short selling with any amount you feel comfortable with. As long as you realize there is a very real possibility that the money you use will be lost, the amount should not matter. You should be aware that commissions and other fees will take a bite out of your profit, making trading with small amounts a costly process, regardless of whether your trades are positive or not. As long as you keep track of your trades and the amounts behind them, you can trade with as little as you would like. A written record should include a running tally of how much you have made or lost so that you can determine whether your new hobby has been good or bad for your pocketbook.

Experienced traders are a different story. These short sellers are not just testing the waters; they are selling short as either a way of supporting themselves, or as a serious tool within their portfolio. As such, they will be trading much larger amounts of money than the beginners. Because short selling can quickly lead to financial ruin, these traders need to have a much tighter grip on their money. A budget or some other form of guidance is necessary to make sure that the proper amount of capital is used with each trade. This will minimize the amount of risk that is faced.

Research

There are many of free research tools out there to help you with your trading. With this in mind, why would anyone want to pay for his or her research tools? Some research companies will have features that the free, and oftentimes minimalist, online sites do not. Many free charts are also wrought with annoying advertisements. If streamlined and efficient research tools are going to help you make a more informed decision, consider paying the extra money for the better product.

Nothing beats old-fashioned research. Whether you are reading an online analysis of a stock or perusing the business section of the newspaper for headlines, you should immerse yourself in your potential portfolio. The broader your knowledge is of market conditions and the more you know about a particular company, the more accurate your opinion will be when it comes time to execute the trade. You will need market knowledge regarding the companies you wish to trade, such as when new products are coming out, when financial reports are to be released, and other fundamental indicators. *The distinction between fundamental and technical analysis is discussed in Chapter 5.*

Whether you decide to pay for that research or whether you have the tenacity to track it down yourself is up to you. If you do decide to look on your own for this information, the many sites already mentioned in this section are good starting points, as is Investopedia (**www.investopedia.com**). Although many individuals use this site strictly as a glossary of financial terms, there are great and timely articles posted for both long and short traders.

Another great research tool is the *Investor's Business Daily*. This daily newspaper tracks a selection of the top performing and underperforming stocks, condensing hours of research into a small, easy-to-use newspaper. Other top newspapers that can be consulted are The Wall Street Journal and the *Financial Times*, although these are not as friendly to short sellers.

Strategy

You should not begin a trade without devising some sort of outline for your trade. This must be a written outline so you will be able to hold yourself accountable down the road and stick to your guidelines. A written strategy should include the following:

- **Reason(s) for entering the trade:** Why does this trade look appealing to you? Why will this be a worthwhile venture?

- **Entry price:** At what point are you willing to enter a trade?

- **Exit price:** What price do you think the stock will bottom out at?

- **Time frame:** How long do you think it will take the stock to find a bottom?

- **Profit:** How much money do you think you will make with this trade?

- **Stop-loss point:** If your trade does not go as planned, at what price do you cut your losses?

It is only after all of this is taken into account that you should begin a trade. At that point, you can calculate how much capital you wish to risk. The appropriate safeguards can then be given to your broker. As mentioned previously, you should not risk more than 1–2 percent of your trading capital on any one trade.

For example: Suppose you are considering shorting 100 shares of Green Mountain Coffee Roasters (GMCR). You are considering the trade because it has just hit its all-time high at just under $90 per share. On top of this, the Bollinger Bands (discussed in Chapter 6) have begun to constrict, which is a strong indicator that the stock is about to undergo a period of volatility. You think that this will be a worthwhile trade because many research firms have recently downgraded the company. Since you believe that the price has hit its resistance level, a reversal has to be right around the corner. The below chart shows GMCR over a two-month period at daily intervals. As you can see, the stock hit its high point at the beginning of February. Since that point, the stock has been at almost a standstill trading at an extremely low volume.

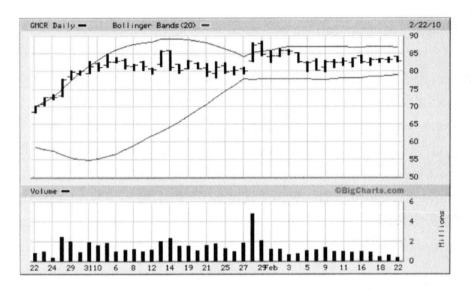

The next piece of the puzzle to consider is when to enter. Obviously you will want to wait until the stock has reached a high that you feel comfortable with. As the stock has dropped from its closing price high of $86.08, the current price, as of February 19, 2010, of $83.01, is a tad too low. This trade is not yet ready to be executed, so you may want to consider a limit order to enter the short sale if and when GMCR reaches $85 even.

The next thing you need to consider is how low you think GMCR will go. At what price are you going to be able to exit this trade with satisfactory profits? In this instance, you think the stock's price will drop down as low as $80.25 over the next week. This takes into account both an exit price and a time frame in which you think the trade will be conducted in. The final thing that you need to take into account is how much you wish to make for the trade. At a drop of $4.75 per share ($85–$80.25), you will be making $475 before commission charges. If this is an acceptable profit to you, and you are confident that the entry and exit points will occur, then by all means, this trade should be executed.

One more thing needs to be considered before the actual execution of the trade. You need to determine at what point the trade has become a lost cause. If the trade does not go as planned, at what price do you abandon the trade? Time has shown that the stock did actually continue to rise after this graph was created, but there was no way to know that based on the above chart. Instead, we would have needed to select a price at which we would be surprised if the stock rose to. If you were to have chosen $88.50 as an exit point, it would have given you a net loss of $3.50 per share for a total loss of $350. As far as losing trades go, this one could have been much worse, especially if a stop-loss point had not been used. In the grand scheme of things, this is a small loss, but a lesson that is important to learn. It is always better to learn your lessons with small amounts rather than thousands of dollars.

Tracking Your Trades

A spreadsheet program makes for a wonderful place to keep this information. Some brokers even market programs that allow you to use stock price charts within a diary. This is a useful tool, especially for the beginning trader because it will allow you to precisely recreate and record the conditions that led to your decision. Again, paying for this option might be well worth the price if it gives you the discipline to better monitor your trades. Although some traders prefer to have all of the modern bells and whistles when it comes to tracking their traders, some traders still prefer the old-fashioned way. Their argument is that by tracking and monitoring your trades by hand, you more fully learn what is going on with the stock and are better able to recognize emerging patterns. Still, this is labor intensive and might not be a task suitable or helpful for everyone.

This list may seem overwhelming at first; there is quite a bit of risk involved with selling stocks short, and because of this, a great deal of preparation should take place before you start. There is no need to worry though. This book is designed to allow you to go at your own pace. If you determine that you need extra practice paper trading, or you just do not feel comfortable with the size of your bankroll, feel free to take as much time as you need before continuing on with the rest of the book.

Risk tolerance

If you are looking to open a short position, undoubtedly, you are looking to find the most profitable trades possible. In order to obtain reliable and consistent returns, you will need to do your homework. While short selling does pose a degree of risk, you will be ameliorating this problem by selecting only stocks of which you are knowledgeable.

Still, there are risks associated with selling short, and you should be made fully aware of what these are prior to opening a position. Before you decide where you want your money to go, ask yourself the following questions:

- *How will I feel if I lose some or all of this money?* Selling a stock short has a high degree of risk involved. Do not enter a trade if you cannot stomach the losses you might face. Either scale back the amount invested, or select a better stock to trade. Regardless of your trading philosophy, if you feel uneasy about a trade, that trade is not for you.

- *Why do I want this trade?* What has attracted you to the trade in the first place? Is it the fact that the stock has risen to a presumably high price that it cannot sustain? Or is the stock in the middle of a trend that you see continuing for the time being? If you are executing the trade for the correct reasons, by all means, go ahead and do so. If, however, you are chasing losses or are executing the trade for some other irrational reason, you will probably not be successful.

- *What are my goals?* You will need to identify all of your goals regarding a trade before entering that trade. Otherwise, how will you know when to end the trade? By setting down your goals in writing, you clearly establish how you want to act during the trade, thus eliminating errors that might occur in the heat of the moment. This is a concept that we will be returning to throughout the course of the book.

Like with any self-run business, there are many factors that need to be taken into account before you will be able to start making money. Consider these things to be start-up costs. Without addressing these issues, you run the risk of trading prematurely. There is a huge possibility that you will be losing money if you are not fully prepared.

Chapter 4

When to Short a Position

W hen to enter a position is one of the most widely debated topics within the trading world. The record will show, however, that there is not one correct answer. Regardless of what various infomercials may tell you, there is no silver bullet system that will allow you to consistently reap the rewards of the stock market. Instead, there are literally hundreds of things to consider and weigh against each other. It is important to remember that even with all these things considered, the market may act the exact opposite of what you expected. Sometimes it even seems like the market has a mind of its own and that there is no way to predict what will happen in the future.

Although when to enter a position is a debatable, when to sell is an even more difficult decision to make. Shorting partially alleviates this problem by making the sell point the entry point. In other words, you are beginning a trade by selling the security first, rather than the traditional long method of buying it. This way, the stress of when to sell is taken away, only leaving the buyback process remaining for the end of the trade. Instead of spending time fretting over exit timing, this part of the trade is already taken care of, allowing you to best determine when to buy back the shares that were shorted. Selling stocks is just as, if not more, important than buying. This is where the money is made and where profits are realized. Successful trading involves both sides, not just buying. By becoming a knowledgeable short seller, you will master the most difficult aspect of trading, and refine both sides of your strategy, whether it is a long or a short position.

What to Take into Account When Opening a Position

The most important consideration to take into account when beginning a trade is the overall state of the market. Is the economy healthy or are people wary that stock prices will continue to drop? The stock market operates in cycles with periods of gains followed by periods of losses. Known as bull and bear periods, the ups and downs (respectively) of the market are affected by the performance of the companies that comprise it. A pronounced downtrend or depression within the market occurs, on average, once every three to five years, the most recent of which occurred beginning in 2008. Crashes also usually occur more quickly than the time it takes for the market to hit a highpoint and typically take longer to recover from. The market does have an overall upward trend though, making short selling an unwise move for long-term investors. But because of its up and downward cycles, selling a stock short can be an excellent way to earn money during the markets' inevitable low points. When looking at the overall state of the market, think about how your proposed trade fits in. Will you be fighting against the current or going with the general trend of the market? These questions will help you see your position in a different light.

If selling a stock is the hardest part of trading, how do short sellers know when to enter a position? There are several factors that need to be taken into account, but there are a few key ones that merit your special attention.

Market timing

When to invest your money is a question that does not have an exact answer. Perfectly timing an entry into the market, regardless of whether it is a long or short position, is extremely difficult and is realistically only achieved by a stroke of luck. Even the best and brightest minds within the financial world have at least a degree of difficulty predicting when an up or downtrend is about to take place. This does not mean it is impossible to predict, but it does require a degree of expertise. The more you learn about the market, the better equipped you will be to realize such things. Although it is impossible to time your entry perfectly, you should still aim for this unattainable goal. As you grow more experienced, you will become — on average — closer and closer to your goal.

Trying to time your short sale just right can lead to ruin for the inexperienced trader; either you will wait too long and miss the opportunity all together, or you will act prematurely and not get the profits you desired. The danger lies in that by trying to time an entry exactly, you are in effect attempting to predict something that has not yet happened. It must be remembered that trading is an inexact science. Basically, you are attempting to predict the highest point that the stock in question is going to hit before beginning a drastic drop. In essence, this approach is no different than playing the lottery. While sudden turnarounds can oftentimes be predicted, there is no way to determine the exact dollar value at which this change will occur.

With that said, there are a couple generic signs that a price reversal is about to occur. The first of these occurs when the stock in question moves up to a short-term highpoint but with significantly low volume. In other words, the stock's price is climbing, but the amount of shares being traded has not increased, so the stock has not captured the attention of the institutional investors that it should have. In this instance, a price reversal may be imminent. Because volume is not very high, trader interest in the stock has not really increased. The gains that a stock sees in this case are usually only illusory. The second warning sign of a price reversal is when the market undergoes a period of "churning," which occurs when a stock's volume goes through an impressive short-term increase but with little to no gains within the price of that stock. When the churning occurs at a highpoint for that particular company's stock, a sell-off usually follows, causing a drastic drop in price.

Rallies can and do occur. You might have seen one of the above warning signs and jumped into the market, selling your stock short with high hopes that it will reverse its price. You might see a few days of lowered prices, and then the stock's price jumps back up. Do not be alarmed by this. Unless the stock starts showing considerable strength for previously unconsidered reason, this type of rally is common. If both the stock's volume and price begin to drastically rise, this is usually a warning sign that a sustained growth is about to occur. But remember, you shorted the stock for a reason. If there is no fundamental change within the company, the rally will probably be short-lived, and your short sale will be safe.

The simplest way to time your entry into a short sale is to wait until the overall market is in a confirmed downtrend due to the fact that stocks are much more likely to drop when this occurs. An overall bearish market will drag almost every stock down with it, especially the new companies that profited most from the preceding bull market. It remains important that you do not sell short at the top of a stock's trend. It is impossible to tell when a stock has reached its peak price — only in retrospect can this be achieved. Instead of trying to time your trade perfectly, wait until the market confirms it is time for a short sale. According to some analysts, such as William J. O'Neil, the founder of the Investor's Business Daily, this does not occur until about six months after a stock has reached its peak. For most cases, you will not need to wait this long. While O'Neil is correct in saying that during bull markets, investors tend to hold on for long periods of time, there are usually signals indicating that a short sale will be profitable prior to his recommended waiting period. Six months is a good waiting period if you plan on a longer-term short sale, but because most short sellers trade over a shorter length of time than this, six months is a bit excessive. Still, this does not mean that you should trade prior to an entry signal.

Insider trading

When most people think of insider trading, they are thinking of the illegal variety. In fact, insider trading occurs often, and as long as certain guidelines are followed, it is completely legal. By definition, an insider is someone who controls 10 percent or more of a company's shares or is an officer or director of the company. Insider trading occurs when one of these individuals buys or sells the stock of the company in question. The people who are most knowledgeable about a stock are the people who work within the structure of the corporation in question. Why would you not take advantage of their knowledge?

There are tight restrictions on these individuals when it comes to the buying and selling of their company's stock. These individuals must be registered within the Securities and Exchange Commission (SEC) and must notify the SEC in advance when they will be placing a trade of their company's stock. Furthermore, insiders may not use information that has not been disclosed to the public as the basis for a trade. When executives are moving large amounts of shares, this can be a good indication that something is happening within the company. This can be either good or bad news, but either way, insiders have a deeper understanding of what their company is experiencing. By paying attention to what they are doing, you too can have that knowledge.

Let us stick with Green Mountain Coffee Roasters Inc. (GMCR) as an example. When Lawrence Blanford, president and CEO of the company, exercised an option on May 27, 2009 to purchase more than 8,000 shares of the GMCR stock at $27.37 per share, it was an indicator of where he thought the market was headed.

The same day that the option was exercised, Blanford sold the same amount of shares for a whopping $85.60 per share. A few days later on June 4th, Blanford exercised another option of more than 8,000 shares for the same $27.37, this time selling the shares for $90.06.

What does this tell us? To the casual observer, it appears as if one of two things happened. Either Blanford's option contract was close to expiring and he wanted to take advantage of the current prices, or he exercised the contract a bit early because he did not think that prices would reach that high in the near future. To take this one step further, if an officer within the company does not think that prices will go beyond that high of a price, how should the rest of us react? Odds are that we should consider shorting that company.

CASE STUDY: DO NOT FIGHT THE TREND

Karl Pierre, founder of Solis LaPierre Corporation, believes that "fighting the market is sure to cause your death." Pierre is based in New York, and he uses short selling as a regular strategy in his everyday trading. He will not fight the market's overall trend, however.

With about 50 percent of his trading volume as short sales, he will only sell a stock short if the overall market is trending downward. This is not as easy as it might sound at first. There are many factors that Pierre considers prior to pulling the trigger on a trade. First of all, he looks for a flag pattern on the stock's price chart. As a day trader, Pierre looks at short-term charts because he is "looking for the quickest fix." Long-term trends are important, but it is the daily ups and downs that most concern him.

There are a few other factors that must be present as well. One is that trading volume must be much higher than usual. This is a signal that institutional investors are acting on a stock. As Pierre states, "Would I want to fish in an empty lake or right on top of a pack of fish so thick that you feel them bumping into your boat as they swim by?" The higher the trading volume, the more active the institutional investors are, thus making the stock all the more attractive. When the professionals are giving a stock their attention, it merits the average trader's attention as well.

Pierre then looks to see where the support line of the stock is. If the stock is too near its support, he abandons the trade; the stock is likely to go through a short-term rally because it is already near its relative low price. The stock is probably going to regain some of its losses as traders buy shares at the temporary discount. This does not mean that the trade is disqualified for future trading. It may, in fact, be a prime candidate for a short sale later that same day.

Lastly, Pierre will look to make sure that the stock is near its short-term high to ensure as much of a profit as possible. It is only after the stock meets all of these criteria that he will execute the trade.

Determining a stock's value

While many people confuse the terms "price" and "value" by using them interchangeably, it is actually a costly mistake. The price of the stock is determined by the amount of money that a single share sells for on the market; this is the dollar amount that you will see on stock charts and reports. The value of a stock, on the other hand, is a more abstract number. *Chapter 5 discusses the many ways to calculate this number.* Basically, this number tries to determine approximately what a stock should be priced at rather than what the actual price is. By taking into account earnings reports, total outstanding debts, and other financial status markers of a company, traders will try to determine what the stock is actually worth. For example when a company has a high debt to net worth ratio, it can be used as a signal to short the stock. When a company has a large amount of debt, it is usually a sign that the company is not performing well. If the stock is trading at a high price, but has little value, the stock becomes a good candidate for a short sale. While this is not always the case, it is true often enough that it must be given some merit. Establishing that these conditions exist is one of the primary tasks of fundamental analysis.

This process takes one major thing for granted: Stock prices fluctuate in a logical manner. In other words, the variations in a stock price occur for a reason other than mere chance. If the public knows that a stock has a low value but a high price, then this would be an indicator that the stock's price is about to drop.

Selecting a Stock

A general rule of thumb when choosing which corporations to sell short is the old idiom that "the bigger they are, the harder they fall." Following this, the companies that saw the biggest gains during the preceding bull market are usually the best candidates for those about to fall once the market turns bearish. Apple Inc.'s stock (AAPL) is a prime example of this, and is, in fact, a company discussed several times throughout this book. In early January 2008, Apple Inc. was hovering around $200 per share. When the housing bubble burst later that year, the entire stock market was eventually affected, including technology stocks. By January 2009, Apple Inc. had been cut in half to under $100 per share.

Small-capitalization stocks are much more dangerous to trade with than large-cap stocks. This is because the small-cap stocks are prone to a greater degree of fluctuation. If a stock trades at a low dollar amount, and a large amount of money is pumped into that stock, the price rise within the stock is going to be much more than if the same amount of money was put into a stock that traded at a higher dollar amount. For example, if a trader bought 1 million shares from a corporation that traded at 10 million shares per day, the company would have increased its volume by 10 percent. If the same 1 million shares were purchased from a company that traded 100 million shares per day, the volume would have increased by only 1 percent. The percentage of change between the two different stocks is extremely different.

Another prime example is the dot-com bubble that occurred during the end of the 20th century and lasted through the beginning of the 21st century. Technology stocks were growing at a breakneck pace. Even companies with little tangible assets were selling at unheard of high prices. When the bubble finally burst, these companies fell and fell hard. Many investors lost millions during the crash, but there were warning signs that could have prevented this. Although these signs are more apparent in retrospect, they were still there to some extent. Many of the Internet and technology stocks that crashed had little in the way of earnings yet were trading for hundreds of dollars per share. The corporations were overextended and had no way to back the profits that their stocks were supposedly reflecting. Because these companies were being purchased at such high prices and had so little in terms of assets, they were poised to eventually crash.

This does not mean that a short seller should have acted right away during the dot-com bubble. On the contrary, if shares were sold short in 1995, the trader would have lost a great deal before the crash finally occurred in 2000. It is vital that warning signs trigger any short sale because there needs to be some sort of imminent happening on the horizon before you act. Remember, you are not trying to foresee the future; rather, you should be acting on the evidence provided. Just because technology stocks were overextended during the dot-com bubble does not mean that it was right to short them right away. As you will see, you do not want to tie up capital for long periods of time in a stagnant investment. This may mean a loss of a few percentage points when it comes to profit, but that is much more acceptable than losing 200–300 percent.

Although they are more risky, small-capitalization stocks oftentimes will provide a great opportunity for short sellers. Because they are so easily affected by market conditions, small-cap stocks can drop sharply during bear markets. As a short seller, these drastic drops in price can be extremely beneficial. Be aware though, the opposite is also true. During bull markets, these stocks can rise just as rapidly.

The short seller must wait for warning signals to be provided to them prior to acting. Whether these signals come from your technical or fundamental analysis does not matter; either way, you still need some sort of confirmation that your move will be the correct one. *Some of these signals have been discussed in the "Market timing" section.* Again, you do not want to try and time a short sale from the stock's absolute highest price. This is a guessing game and will result in a loss more often than not. Instead, wait for the signs to say it is time. Sometimes this will occur several months after the peak. This is due to the fact that there are always residual buyers of a stock in a bull trend. These buyers are hoping to catch a small piece of the profits yet are a bit late to the party.

Instead, all they accomplish is prolonging the plateau at the top of the charts. The stock has begun to show signs that it is weakening although not everyone may have realized this. You will want to wait until this bullish behavior subsides before you make your move, and there are mathematical ways to determine when this point occurs. *This will be discussed in greater detail in Chapter 6.*

Bankruptcy

The most ideal situation when you enter a short position is to see the company's stock price fall down to zero. This happens when a company files for bankruptcy. However, there may be a delay in between the filing for bankruptcy and the actual bottoming out of the stock's price. This was the case with the Enron scandal; the company filed bankruptcy on December 2, 2001, yet there was still quite a bit of speculative trading activity before the company finally went belly-up.

In a perfect world, you will be looking for companies that face the risk of going bankrupt. Because of the fact that bond holders are repaid prior to shareholders, looking at bond rates can be an effective way of predicting bankruptcy. Bonds are traded regularly on the open market; knowing their current value as compared to their purchase price is a valuable tool for short sellers. Analyst Henry Miller states that a short sale candidate should have its bonds be trading at 60 cents per dollar or lower. When the bond reaches a price of 40 cents per dollar or lower, it is almost inevitable that the company will file bankruptcy.

Bankruptcy is only filed when a company faces the inability to pay off its debts. If a company has little debt, no matter how poorly it might appear to be doing, bankruptcy is not as likely.

When looking at the likelihood of bankruptcy, focus on companies with a high debt to wealth ratio.

There are two types of bankruptcy to be aware of: Chapter 7 and Chapter 11. **Chapter 7 bankruptcy** indicates that the company is largely beyond help. The financial problems faced are too large to overcome. If a company files Chapter 7, it is a good indication that assets will be liquidated and creditors will have their borrowed money partially returned.

Chapter 11 bankruptcy, on the other hand, allows the company to go through what is known as reorganization. A court judge will monitor this process and the company officials will submit a plan as to how they intend to revive the company. Both of these options usually spell the same result for shareholders: The price of their shares is about to be decimated.

Companies are required to file a financial report once each fiscal quarter. For quarterly reports, companies have 45 days after the end of the quarter; for yearly reports they have 90 days. If a company is delayed in filing such a report, it can be a dead giveaway that there are internal problems within the company.

Do not fall in love with any one trade

Do not sell short because it is a good trade; do it because it is the best trade. The market is huge and opportunities present themselves several times every day. If there is doubt or uneasiness with a particular trade, simply stay away from it. There are far too many excellent trades for you to act upon than to be wasting your time with mediocre ones.

Keeping a written journal, either on a spreadsheet or in a notebook, will be beneficial to you. By tracking each and every trade you make and recording the thought process that went into the trade, you will have a better idea of what works and what does not work. People have their own strengths and weaknesses, and the sooner you identify yours as a trader the better you will be. A written record will also help you better understand what factors are most important in a successful trade, and which factors are not as meaningful. Ranking your trades on a scale of 1 to 10 may also be of benefit to you. It will help you whittle down the less enthusiastic trades and focus on the top trades.

Sample Journal Entry

I started watching Green Mountain Coffee Roasters Inc. (GMCR) several months ago in anticipation of a long position. When the stock gapped up a few days later in response to an earnings report, I knew I had missed the boat. Instead of buying late, I decided to wait. Now, it looks like the company is having trouble maintaining current high prices. While it probably will not fall all the way down to past prices, it looks it has hit its resistance level.

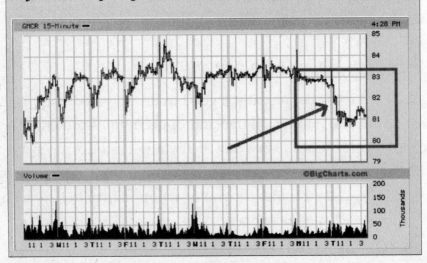

> *The point at which I entered this trade is indicated with the ar-*
> *row. I entered this trade a bit late; I had not expected the stock to*
> *gap down as much as it did opening on Tuesday. Rather than the*
> *$83.50 to $83.75 that I had hoped for, I got in at $81.95. I have*
> *set up a stop-loss point at $83.50 and will cover my position for*
> *a profit at $80.25.*

Written records combined with a ranking system will also in-crease your self-discipline in regards to trading. If you are being held accountable for your trades, even if it yourself that is doing the accounting, you will be less likely to take on poorly thought out positions.

Sure, specializing in a specific trade will benefit you, but you do not want to become so specialized that you lose sight of the mar-ket's other attributes. Perhaps you have found a sector that you love or maybe you have discovered a certain company that is extremely volatile. However, you could be missing out on an-other, equally as volatile company or sector within the market. You should also never completely discount one type of analysis over the other. The most successful traders are able to look at the indicators they find most valuable, and then cross-reference them with other indicators. Looking at a company's fundamentals is great, but if you are unaware of its price history, you will be miss-ing out on half the picture. The same is true with any stance you can take. Never forget how vast the market is. You will never completely understand it, just when you begin to think you have a particular type of trade mastered, something will change, and you will be back at square one. The best you can hope for is to understand it enough to have consistent profits.

Before exiting a position

You have selected the stock and pulled the trigger. The stock you have chosen has indeed declined in price and is beginning to make you a profit. Now comes the hard part: How do you know when the ride is over? How do you know when to buy back the shares and return them to the broker to cover your position?

If you are using a system, this question will already have been answered for you. You cover your position when the stock reaches the price that was predetermined before you began the trade. You can either select this by hand or rely on your computer program to do it for you. Where the number comes from does not matter as much as the fact that if you are using a system, you need to follow it as closely as possible. This may mean setting a limit order to exit the position for you automatically once that price is achieved.

Most will be using a discretionary method, however, and will not have a concrete number to go against. Still, we should have a general idea of how far the stock will reasonably sink. One key feature to use as a reference is the stock's intrinsic value. What is the stock really worth? By calculating the price per share where you think the company's shares should realistically be selling, you are setting a lower boundary for yourself. If you are riding a simple price reversal, this might be a short distance away from the starting point. If the company is inherently flawed, you will be looking at a longer drop. Or, what if the opposite occurred and the stock has increased in price? Barring any sort of concrete system, the exit point will again be left to your discretion. If you have not set a stop-loss point for yourself, you will have to determine when to admit defeat and take the loss. This is one of the hardest things to do in selling a stock short but also one of the most important. Admitting failure to yourself is not an easy task, but remember that you will have failed trades. Everybody does. If you minimize these losses, you will be maximizing your earnings.

If this is the case, what you thought the stock's true pricing was and what the market viewed it as were two different things. Then, you will need to evaluate ending the trade on a case-by-case basis. How much capital is at risk? How much have you lost so far? How long has the trade been open? What is your comfort level with where the trade has gone?

Sometimes, your timing will not be perfect. Maybe you have initiated the trade on Monday, but come Friday the stock has not yet declined in price. This is common because stocks do not always act the way we expect them to. Again, your actions should be determined by the research you have put into the trade and your comfort level. If you do not mind that the stock's price has risen by $1–$2, and you are still convinced that the stock is bound to drop in price, by all means stick with the trade. One of the great things about discretionary trading, however, is that you have the ability to "feel out" a trade. If you are uncomfortable with where the trade has headed, you can always end the trade. Just make sure that you are not letting your emotions cloud your decision making process.

Chapter 5
Fundamental and Technical Analysis

Fundamental and technical analysts have been debating for years over which method is better equipped to pick winning stocks. Both try to accomplish the same thing though: predict the future of a stock's price. Their methods for doing so, however, differ drastically. Even the best fundamental analysts take a stock's current and past prices into account. The best technical analysts know a thing or two about a company's inner workings. Although the strategies differ, a good trader understands and uses elements from both camps. As already mentioned, there is no one best way of looking at a stock. For some it is strictly fundamental or technical analysis that they rely on. Still others use some varying combination of the two. By at least being aware of both trains of thought, you are increasing your knowledge of how the market operates — this will never be a bad thing.

Fundamental Analysis

Fundamental analysis is the study of a company's core inner workings. There are many factors taken into account, but they boil down to one key factor: predicting future profits by using a sort of snap shot of the company's fiscal health. A company's overall strengths and weaknesses are analyzed and quantified through fundamental analysis. As with any information, you should compare the numbers found through fundamental analysis to other companies' numbers within the same sector. This will let you know what the industry standard is and allow you to compare where that particular company ranks amongst the companies that share similar traits.

Both macroeconomic and microeconomic factors must be considered when examining a stock using fundamental analysis. So, the larger market conditions and smaller company issues should be looked at. Looking at just a particular company is useless if you do not understand how it is performing relative to the other companies it is competing against or how the current issues affecting the company will shape future decisions. Both the big and the little picture must be given an examination. Issues such as jobless claims, national debt, federal interest rates, and the overall direction of current stock market all are macroeconomic factors that influence companies on the microeconomic scale. Obviously, during a time of high unemployment rates there will be less discretionary spending, and thus less activity in the stock market. The more you know about these overlaying conditions, the better prepared you will be to deal with companies on a one-on-one basis.

There are many factors that fundamental analysts weigh when determining whether to enter a position, all of which are used to try and predict where a company's stock is headed. Profits, past and future, are looked at, as well as products manufactured or marketed by the company, and how experts think those products will perform for the company. Outstanding debts are also taken into consideration: How and when is the company planning on paying these debts? How is the capital acquired through loans, whether they are bank or bond loans, used to make a profit for the company? These factors and more are all part of fundamental analysis. The following terms are some of the more important measurements that analysts use when examining a company.

Earnings per share

The earnings per share is the most basic measurement of a company and tells how much the company in question's share value has gone up or down over a specified period of time. While it may not seem like an important factor, the length of time is essential so that a correct view can be taken of the company. Amounts of outstanding shares may vary from day to day, making it necessary to either take an average or a snapshot of sorts regarding the company's fiscal strength. The EPS can also give traders an idea of how quickly the company's stock has increased or decreased over a period of time. EPS is calculated with the following equation:

$$\frac{\text{Net income} - \text{Dividends on preferred stock}}{\text{Number of outstanding shares}}$$

The amount of shares outstanding is not easy to calculate. With some large companies having tens of millions of shares being traded each day, it is difficult to be exact with this number. Analysts will use one of two methods to approximate this number then. The first is by simply taking a snapshot of the stock. How many shares are outstanding at a given moment? What are current net profits? These numbers are pretty accurate, but they do not mean much if you are trying to determine EPS over a period of time. The second method is calculated by taking a weighted average of the stock, giving a more accurate picture of the stock over time. By looking at numbers over a given time period, the company's value over time can be approximated more precisely than with a single snapshot.

As far as short sellers are concerned, EPS is an extremely valuable tool. An expanding company will have a high EPS and will often-times outperform the market as a whole. However, if a company has an outrageously high EPS, it may be a sign that the company is overextended and poised to drop in price. Companies that have expanded too quickly and cannot sustain their market position are exposed this way. This is largely a subjective process; it is hard to tell what is too high of an EPS without looking at the company's other fundamental indicators. It is also a way to predict a price correction. If a company's stock price has gone up drastically, yet the EPS is negative, this is often a sign that stock prices are about to drop.

Price/earnings ratio

A close cousin to the EPS, the price/earnings (P/E) ratio determines how closely a stock's price follows its actual earnings per share. The higher the P/E ratio, the more investors and traders are anticipating that a stock's price will continue to rise. As the P/E ratio of a stock starts to fall, market prices will soon follow suit. Price-to-earnings is calculated by the following formula:

$$\frac{\text{Market price per share}}{\text{EPS}}$$

As you can see, this formula takes into account both the actual price of the stock and the estimated EPS. If a weighted average is used, time is also taken into account.

There are two main types of P/E ratios that are used by analysts. The trailing P/E will give you an idea of how the stock has performed over the past, while the forward P/E is based off of future estimated earnings. Obviously, the trailing P/E is going to be more accurate than the forward P/E ratio because one relies on historical prices while the other relies on estimated future prices, but it is not always the most beneficial indicator. Because it relies on past data, it does not take into account future earnings. If a company is expected to become less profitable over time, its forward P/E will go up as the EPS loses value. Short traders can use a rising P/E as a signal to set up a potentially profitable trade. When a stock's P/E ratio climbs, it is an indicator that either market price is going up or that the EPS is going down. While a P/E of 10:15 used to be considered reasonable, today companies can safely operate at a higher P/E without running into trouble. Still, if the P/E is too high when compared to the other fundamental indicators, it is a good sign that prices are about to fall.

Return on assets

The return on assets (ROA) measurement is a calculation of a company's efficiency of use of tangible assets. The ROA does not show how the stock is performing in the stock market; rather it shows how well the company is performing for retail customers. It is calculated by the following formula:

$$\frac{\text{Net income} + \text{Interest expense}}{\text{Total assets}}$$

After tax earnings (your net income plus interest expense) divided by total assets gives the trader a look at how efficient a corporation is. As ROA increases, the company is using its assets more profitably and indicates the company is financially sound. The opposite is also true; a falling ROA means that a company is not earning as much as it could be through customer-based revenue and, if it has not occurred already, its stock may be about to drop. It is important that a company performs well in the stock market, but if the company does not fulfill customer needs, it is going to fail eventually.

Return on equity

The return on equity (ROE) indicator proves to be much more useful to technical analysts who make their decisions by looking at stock prices, thanks to the fact that it takes a company's profitability from shareholders into account as well. This measurement is calculated with the following formula:

$$\frac{\text{Post-tax earnings}}{\text{Shareholder equity}}$$

This formula calculates the amount of profit that a company generates with the profit that is acquired from the money invested by shareholders. A low ROE indicates that a company is not properly using their liquid assets and is therefore a good candidate for a short position.

Debt/equity ratio

The debt/equity ratio is another indicator of a company's fiscal health. This is the equivalent of a credit report for a company and is a measure of the company's leverage in terms of the capital available to the company versus the capital being used. The debt/equity ratio is:

$$\frac{\text{Total liabilities}}{\text{Shareholders' equity}}$$

One would think that the less debt a company has, the better. But a low debt/equity ratio is not necessarily a good thing. It can be an indicator that a company is not making the best use of its spending power. Just as credit report companies frown upon someone who does not use at least a portion of the credit available to them, companies can actually miss out on opportunities if they are not using the credit available to them in order to help with expansion efforts.

Another shortcoming of the debt to equity ratio is that it often does not take interest into account. Loans from institutional lenders and bonds taken out by investors all need to be repaid plus any interest that accumulates. Additionally, a company's shares may be overvalued, meaning that the company is not actually as financially healthy as it looks on paper. This would artificially lower the debt/equity ratio and mislead investors who have not taken such things into account while looking at this measurement. Short sellers need to be aware of these things because they can make an otherwise decent trade turn sour. If you are looking at a company with a favorable debt-to-equity ratio and decide not to sell it short, you might be in for an unpleasant surprise when the company suddenly falls in price, the exact opposite of what you predicted. This could occur if a company does not use its leverage properly.

Market capitalization

A stock's market capitalization is a reference to the amount of dollars and shares traded. There is no specific amount that separates a large-cap stock from a medium- or small-cap stock. However, there are some loosely agreed upon numbers that help determine how a specific stock is sized up. A stock with a market cap under $2 billion is considered a small-cap company, a medium-cap company has a valuation of roughly $2 billion to $10 billion, and large-cap stocks are valued at more than $10 billion. Obviously, these numbers fluctuate on a daily basis, so there is some blurring of the boundaries for companies that rest in between two market cap levels. Market capitalization is determined by the following formula:

$$\text{Number of shares X Price per share}$$

So, a $10 stock with 10 million outstanding shares would have a market cap of $100 million and would thus be considered a small-cap stock. The main fault with market capitalization, and what makes it so hard to define, is the fact that these numbers change daily. As prices fluctuate and shares are bought and sold making the price of stock vary, the market capitalization of a stock changes. Because of this, it is hard to determine if borderline companies qualify as large, middle, or small cap stocks. As stated previously, small-cap stocks tend to be more volatile than large-cap stocks because they respond more dramatically to consumer sentiment. This might make small-cap stocks excellent trades for a day trader but not so helpful for position traders. Knowing your niche within the market becomes very important when looking at a company's capitalization.

Projected earnings growth

The projected earnings growth of a stock is a prediction of where the company's stock is going to be at some point in the future. Common measurements take into account both quarterly and yearly growth. A company's projected earnings growth (PEG) is determined by the following formula:

$$\frac{\text{P/E ratio}}{\text{Projected growth in earnings}}$$

Companies that are predicted to grow often will, but not necessarily because of a favorable change within their fundamental indicators. By a sort of placebo effect, companies often grow because investors think they are supposed to. This makes sense, though, because if you think a company is going to grow, you will invest your money into the company's stock, which creates more demand for the stock and less supply, which leads to an increase in price. Because of this placebo effect, a high projected earnings growth number does not necessarily spell doom for short sellers. It should, at the very least, be a warning to carefully check other fundamental indicators to make sure that the professionals and analysts who predict the projected earnings growth do not see something within the company that you may have overlooked.

By looking at a stock's EPS in addition to this indicator, you will see what a company's current position is in comparison to its projected future. If the two do not seem to coincide, the company may be having problems. For example, if a company has a high EPS, but a low PEG, analysts think that the company's productivity is going to slacken. The company may be doing well presently, as judged by its EPS, but analysts do not expect this trend to continue, hence the low PEG. Just as the placebo effect can raise stock prices, this divergence can cause a sell off that will force stock prices to fall.

Price/sales ratio

The price/sales ratio compares what the stock's market capitalization price is to how much the company earns over a given time period. The price-to-sales ratio is calculated using the following formula:

$$\frac{\text{Share Price}}{\text{Revenue over a 12-month timeframe}}$$

This is a valuable way to approximate whether the price of the stock is where its value says it should be. A range of the previous 12 months is used to calculate the second number in this ratio. Although the price/sales ratio is a useful tool, it is limited because it does not take into account a company's outstanding expenses, debts, and liabilities. These factors can adversely affect a company's stock price if an earnings report or some other event exposes these deficiencies. A company is considered overvalued if its price-to-sales ratio is at or more than 3.

Price/book ratio

The price/book ratio is another way to attempt to quantify a comparison between a stock's trading price and its intrinsic value. It is calculated by the following formula:

$$\frac{\text{Stock price}}{\text{Total assets - Intangible assets and liabilities}}$$

This formula gives traders an idea of whether a stock is overvalued; it is trading at a price much higher than the stock is actually worth. An extremely high price/book ratio is often a sign that a stock has been overbought and that a correction is about to occur, often resulting in a good opportunity for short sellers.

Beta

Beta is a measure of a stock's volatility. It can be used in reference to another company, the sector that the corporation exists in, or the overall market. The beta of a certain stock will be given to you on stock exchange Web sites because it is a somewhat complex calculation using regression analysis. With this regression model, the stock's performance during market swings is calculated. A beta of 1 is an indication that the stock keeps in step consistently with the comparison index, a beta of greater than 1 means that the stock is more volatile than the comparison, and likewise, a beta lower than 1 is a signal that it is less volatile. The higher the degree of volatility within a stock's price, the more likely it is that the stock will experience wild ups and downs giving it a high beta. While by no means does a high rate of volatility guarantee that a stock will drop in price, it is just more likely to do so than a stock with little volatility.

Accumulation/distribution

The accumulation/distribution is a simple indicator with a complex mathematical formula. The equation compares supply and demand in light of a stock's high and low price for a given time period. It also will determine whether there is a divergence between a stock's price and its volume. See the formula below:

$$\frac{(\text{Stock's closing price} - \text{Low price}) - (\text{Stock's high price} - \text{Closing price})}{(\text{Stock's high price} - \text{Low price}) \times \text{Volume for given period}}$$

What the long equation calculates is simply how supply and demand intersect. This indicator shows whether traders are accumulating shares (buying) or distributing their shares (selling).

In order to get a better understanding of this indicator, consider once again the stock of Apple Inc. (AAPL). On Jan. 8, 2010, Apple Inc. shares closed at $211.98 per share after hitting a low of $209.06 and a high of $212.00. Its volume stood at 15,995,583 shares traded over the course of the day. The formula would then look like this:

$$\frac{(211.98 - 209.06) - (212 - 211.98)}{(212 - 209.06) \text{ X } 15,995,583}$$

The result is 0.0000000617 accumulation/distribution for the day, which by itself means nothing to traders. If you look at this compared to another company within the computer/technology sector you gain a better understanding of how Apple is performing. By looking at the Palm Inc. (PALM) accumulation/distribution for the day, we gain a bit of insight into how each company stands in comparison to the other.

$$\frac{(12.43 - 10.96) - (12.44 - 12.43)}{(12.44 - 10.96) \text{ X } 28,381,088}$$

Palm Inc., one of Apple's biggest competitors, performed at a much higher volume than Apple Inc. did on the same day. But as you can see, its prices per share are not nearly as high as Apple Inc. With a result of 0.0000000348, you can see that its accumulation/distribution number is also much lower. This is mainly because of the higher volume that Palm Inc. traded at over the course of the day. As mentioned previously, a large volume with little price change is called churning and is often an indicator that a stock's price is about to drop. The lower the accumulation/distribution number is, the more their shares are being sold, rather than being bought. *Accumulation/distribution can also be charted on a graph as a technical indicator and will be covered later in this chapter.*

What Does it All Mean?

Determining the meaning behind the numbers calculated is only beneficial if they are used in comparison to the company's industry standard. The Apple Inc. and Palm Inc. comparison is a prime example. Apple and Palm are both technology companies with similar products. However, Apple has recently left Palm in the dust thanks to the iPhone and the iPod. You can see that a firm grasp on which products each company offers as far as a product line goes is necessary as well as how these products are going to be received by the public. This is a type of fundamental analysis.

If Apple did not come out with these products, Palm may very well be a much more profitable stock. The PalmPilot PDA (personal digital assistant) was a revolutionary product when it was first released in 1996, yet these models were eclipsed when the iPhone was released in 2007. If you were to have taken a long position in Palm at the end of 2008, you would have seen a rise of about 10 points per share over the next year, which is by no mean a disreputable gain. Apple, in comparison, rose by more than 100 points during the same time period as its new product gained in popularity. If you were to have taken a short position in Apple, not knowing about the release of these key products, you would have lost a substantial amount of money. Fundamental analysts need to know the company they are trading inside and out in order to avoid such a catastrophe.

Technical Analysis

Technical analysis is the study of a stock's past market activity through the use of charts. Visually, this is a much easier aspect of trading to understand than a stock's fundamentals. A stock's price and its change over time are the main pieces of data used within technical analysis, but volume and volatility are also amongst the many other factors that are used to calculate the charts technical analysts use. Technical analysis relies on the premise that past prices and trends influence a stock's future actions.

Many short-term traders, especially short sellers, rely solely on technical analysis because it is great for detecting trends within a stock's movement patterns. This makes it a wonderful tool for day traders who wish to cash in on the slight ups and downs within a stock's price. However, technical analysis is only part of the puzzle. Fundamental analysis is just as important, especially for longer-term short selling, and a firm understanding of both will help you over the short and long term.

Volume

The volume of a stock is a term for the amount of shares traded over a given time period, usually one day. This gives traders a rough idea of a stock's volatility. Companies with large volumes usually see less fluctuation in their stock since small changes in trading volume will not affect the price as much. Disconnects between price and volume can spell future trouble for a stock's price. A decline in a stock's volume is sometimes a predecessor of price declines. When volume begins to drop it is often a signal of problems within the fundamentals of the stock. When traders and investors begin to lose interest in a stock, it means that it is not being traded as much. Volume, in this respect, symbolizes the strength of the stock. Stock prices will go through their biggest periods of change when volume is at its highest. Remember, this can go both ways. If the volume of the stock starts to rise and the price is dropping, this can be a signal that the stock's price is about to reverse and become bullish. Short sellers should avoid a bullish stock since this type of stock is either already rising or about to rise in price. A stock's volume tends to be higher right at the opening of the trading day, and then again at the end of the day. Lulls in the middle of the day are common, even amongst the most highly traded companies.

Volume is what drives price. A stock cannot go through a price change if there are no shares being bought or sold. In other words, without a catalyst, stock prices will remain stagnant.

Momentum

A stock's momentum is a study of change in price in light of how quickly that change takes place. If there is a discrepancy between a stock's momentum and its price progression, this can equal trouble for the stock because a drop in price is likely at some point in the future. However, these changes do not necessarily take place right away. Divergences between price and momentum on a chart can take place for quite a while before a reversal takes place, so momentum is more of a long-term predictive tool. Momentum can also be a measure of a stock's integrity. The momentum will expose any overbought or oversold conditions that the stock may be facing.

Momentum is measured by several different methods. The **Moving Average Convergence/ Divergence (MACD)** indicator is a widely used formula that can be used to measure a stock's momentum over the course of time. Although this indicator will sometimes predict price reversals, it oftentimes does not show a reversal until shortly after the fact. As a momentum oscillator, the MACD acts as a predictor for the ups and downs of a stock's price. There are several things that the MACD indicates, and because of this, there are a couple different lines that comprise the MACD. The first line is the MACD line, which you can calculate by subtracting the 26-day exponential moving average from the 12-day exponential moving average. Because different time periods are cited, although some of the same days will be referenced, they will have different weightings. The second line is called the signal line and is calculated by using a nine-day exponential moving average. The signal line moves similarly to the MACD line because, again, it has some of the same days comprising it. These two lines give traders quite a bit of information. The first is what type of trend the stock is currently experiencing. If the MACD line crosses to go above the signal line, it is considered evidence that an upward trend is beginning, with a price increase usually to follow. If it crosses below the signal line, then a downtrend may be about to occur.

On balance volume, another momentum indicator, is a process that assumes that past volume measurements will indicate future price changes. To calculate the on balance volume, analysts take the days where a stock's price rises and add their values together. On the days where stocks drop in price, their volume is subtracted from the total.

For example, assume that a stock has risen consistently for six days and has had 10 million shares traded. The on balance volume would then equal 10 million. On the seventh day, the stock drops slightly in value and sells 1 million shares. This brings the on balance volume down to 9 million.

A steadily falling on balance volume will be an indicator that a stock's price is also falling. Whether this is a trend cannot usually be determined by the on balance volume measurement. Other indicators are better equipped to do this. Trends and trend reversals, on the other hand, are better anticipated with moving averages. Good software packages will give you access to several other different types of momentum-based indicators such as moving averages, MACD lines, and stochastic oscillators.

Simple and exponential moving averages

A simple moving average is a method of tracking trends within a price chart. Again, this indicator tries to predict when a price reversal is about to occur. This can be used to calculate both long and short periods of time; 18 days is perhaps the most popular indicator amongst traders, thanks to the fact that it is a relatively short measurement of time. One key thing to take note of is the fact that the longer the time period being measured, the less affected the chart will be by the inevitable daily changes. The moving average is made up of price trends over a given time period. The direction of the moving average line will be a dead giveaway of the current trend the stock is experiencing. If you are a momentum trader, this indicator is going to become your best friend as it will be a solid indicator of the direction the stock is currently trending.

The simple moving average is shown as a line that appears over a price chart. When the simple moving average line crosses the price line to go underneath it, this is an indicator that the stock may go up in price. If the opposite occurs and the simple moving average line goes above the price line this may indicate that the stock is weakening. The following for Apple (AAPL) shows an 18-day simple moving average; note how the price bars interact with the line.

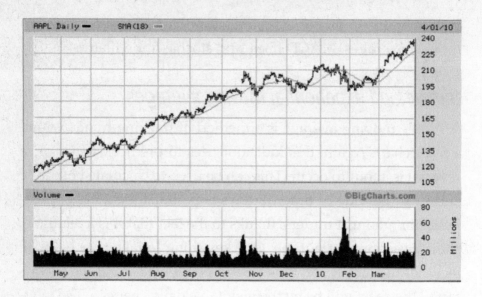

At the far right of the chart, the price seems to be about $15 more than the moving average line; only time will tell if this will results in a price correction.

The exponential moving average is similar to the simple moving average, except that days are weighted differently. While a simple moving average counts each day equally, an exponential moving average gives the most recent days more importance and the further back you go, the days become less important. The below chart is again for AAPL, this time with an exponential moving average of 18 days.

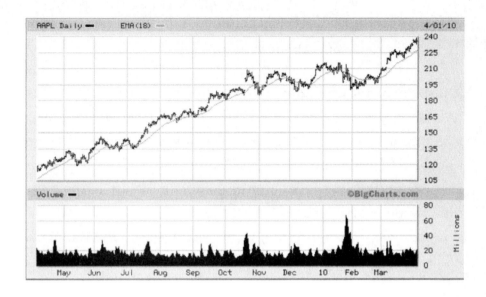

The exponential moving average line in this chart appears to be a bit lower than in the simple moving average chart as it approaches the far right of the chart. This chart can be considered a stronger signal that the stock is about to level out.

Stochastic oscillators

A stochastic oscillator measures the effect of buying and selling by evaluating a stock's momentum. Based on the fact that stock prices oscillate frequently, stochastic oscillators attempt to predict when a stock is overbought or oversold, and thus ready to go through a price reversal. This type of indicator works because stochastic oscillators take into account the movement of a stock's past prices. The premise behind this is that when a stock is in an uptrend, it will close each day at a price near the high for that day. When it is in a downtrend, it will close near its daily low. This becomes a useful tool because when the stock is in an uptrend and begins closing near its daily low, it is a good indication that a price reversal is about to occur.

A **fast stochastic oscillator** covers a short time period; the industry standard is usually around 5 days. This measurement takes into account the highest high prices achieved during the time period, as well as the lowest low prices. Opening and closing prices are also referenced so that a more complete picture of the given time frame is arrived at. When the overall trend of the stock is upward, you will notice that share prices close near the highs, while during downtrends, they close near lows.

This assumption helps generate the conclusion that fast stochastic oscillators can predict overbought and oversold conditions. Varying on a scale of 0 to 100, stochastic oscillators generally use a score of 80 or higher to acknowledge that a stock is overbought, and thus a good signal for short sellers to initiate a position. The higher the stochastic reading, the more likely a price drop is about to occur. Because fast stochastic oscillators use such a short period of time for their data, they are extremely sensitive to changes in price. This makes a fast stochastic a great tool for shorter-term traders.

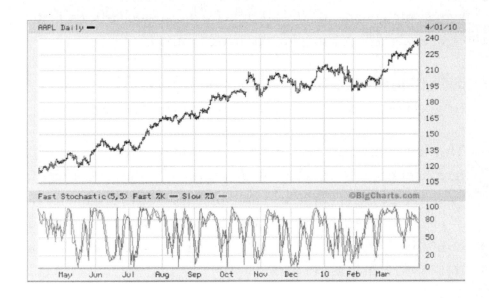

Above, we see the now familiar price chart for AAPL with an additional chart at the bottom. The fast stochastic for Apple shows us that the stock is right around 80, indicating that the stock might be overbought. This is a borderline judgment, though, since the line is so close to the 80 line.

Slow stochastic oscillators are much like their fast brethren, except they measure a longer period of time, usually 14 days, thus making them better for longer-term traders. Because they use more days in their equations, slow stochastic oscillators produce much smoother graphs and are generally more reliable with their buy and sell signals. Stochastic oscillator charts are comprised of two lines: the %K and %D. The %/D line is the most widely followed, but both are extremely important. %D is calculated with a moving average of the past three units of time of the %K line. For example, if %K measures changes over the last 14 days, %D will be calculated by taking a moving average of the three most recent days. When the %K and the %D line cross each other, buy and sell signals are generated. The %K line for a fast stochastic oscillator can be calculated using the following formula:

100 X [(Most recent closing price – Lowest price over last 5 days) X (Highest price over last 5 days – Lowest price over last 5 days)]

The slow stochastic oscillator chart for Apple reveals a much different set of lines. These lines are much smoother and easier to interpret, but it still appears that Apple is hovering right around 80 on the stochastic chart. Before making any decision on whether to short this stock you should probably consult other indicators to see if they are in agreement.

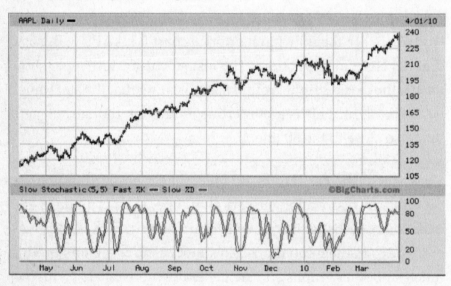

Bollinger bands

Another measure of volatility, Bollinger bands take a stock's standard deviation, which measures how far a stock's price strays from what is expected, into account. The "bands" are signified as two lines that move in accordance with price; the wider apart these lines are, the more volatile the stock is and the more likely a current price change will occur. Analysts use the tightening of bands as a measure that volatility is about to occur. This indicator has a second purpose. If the stock price line nears or touches the top "band," the stock is considered overbought. Overbought conditions often result in price corrections that short sellers can profit off of. The chart below shows Apple's daily chart with Bollinger bands superimposed.

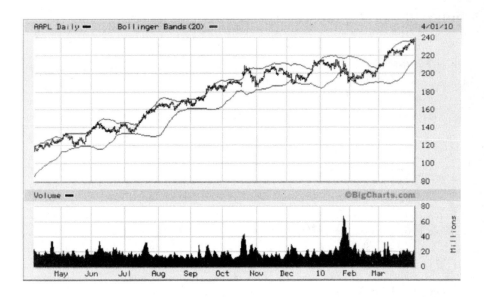

As you can see, when prices approach the top band, they usually do not stay there for very long; this makes the stock a good candidate for a short sale. The reverse is also true; when prices near the bottom band, the price is usually poised to rise. As you can see, the price changes are not always drastic, and they do not always last for long. Still for day traders hoping to cash in on quick profits, this can be a very valuable indicator because of its accuracy in price prediction.

Price channels

A price channel is simply a set of trend lines on either side of a price bar graph. This can be used to predict both long and short-term price reversals for a stock. When the price breaks through the top channel, it is usually an indicator that a drop off is about to occur. The price chart below shows the same price chart for Apple that was used in the Bollinger bands example, but this time with a computer-generated price channel over it.

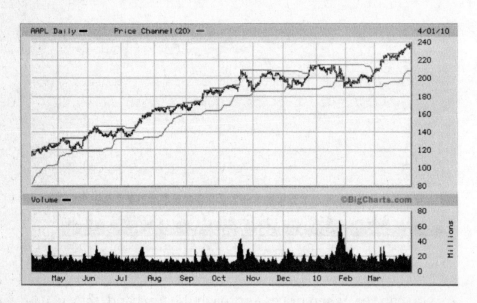

Again, this indicator shows overbought and oversold conditions when the price nears the appropriate channel line. A short sale may be appropriate for traders when the upper channel is breached because prices do not typically stay above the upper price channel line for long.

Relative strength index

The relative strength index (RSI) calculates a number between 0 and 100. This number indicates buying and selling conditions; a high RSI indicates that the stock in question is overbought while a low RSI indicates that a stock is oversold. A high RSI in other-wise weak stocks is very strong indicator that a price is about to drop. RSI is determined by the following formula:

100 – (100 / (1 + (Average of up closes for the day / Average of down closes for the day))

Look at the below chart for Apple. As prices drop from their high near $215 down to $190, notice how the RSI, as indicated in the bottom portion of the graph, drops from around 80 to 40.

The industry average is between 70 and 80 when it comes to overbought conditions, and Apple's two-month chart is a great example of this. Once the RSI levels out at around 80, the RSI quickly begins dropping, creating an excellent opportunity for swing trading short sellers.

Which Indicators Should You Use?

Technical indicators can be overwhelming. There are so many of them, and most have multiple variations that can be plugged in as well. How do you know which ones to use?

This is a tough question because some indicators work better depending on your personal trading style. Practice and trial and error are probably the only ways to truly figure out which indictors will give you the most benefit. Most experts agree that you should only use a few technical indicators at a time; otherwise, it is just too overwhelming. This will keep your charts simple and will help you stay focused on the indicators that will truly benefit you. For example, if you are a momentum trader, moving averages will be more beneficial to you than the stock's relative strength index. This occurs because moving averages operate by confirming the current trend of a stock. The relative strength index, on the other hand, tries to predict future movement.

Many technicians use the MACD indicator on a separate chart placed directly below the price chart, with some sort of breakout indicator on the top price chart. Price channels are a popular predictor. Take a look at the sample chart of IBM on the next page:

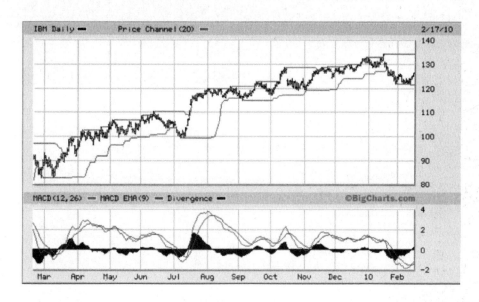

This is a basic bar price chart for the past year of IBM's daily prices with a price channel superimposed and a MACD graph below. As you can see there are several different activities contained within this chart. The top of the chart shows a stock skirting the lower half of its price channel, while the bottom MACD graph looks like a bearish phase is coming to an end. Because these indicators hint that prices are about to rise, IBM is probably not the best stock to short at this particular moment.

 The type of indicators you select are largely determined by your personal style of learning. Are you a visual learner? If so, technical analysis will probably be your method of choice. If you learn more by doing, calculating a company's fundamentals will probably be better for you. You will be selecting the indicators within these broader categories using trial and error. This is one of the reasons paper trading is a vital part of your platform.

Chapter 6

Charts Made Simple

There has been much mention of graphs and charts throughout this book so far, but without an explanation of what the charts are actually showing, they would mean little. You can sculpt a chart to look however you want by manipulating the length of time and the dates examined alongside with which measurement you choose to look at. This is why guidance is necessary when examining charts. Many successful short sellers use charts as part of their process for selecting which stocks to act upon, and when to execute and subsequently end a trade. There are three main types of charts:

- A **line chart** is the most basic form of a chart. It also contains the least amount of information for traders. It will show only the closing prices for the given time period.

- A **bar chart** will give quite a bit more information than a line chart. Aside from just showing closing prices, the bar chart also will show opening, high, and low prices for the given time period as well.

- The **candlestick charting** method will give the trader the most amount of information. It includes all of the parts of a bar chart but also has the addition of the main trading range for the day. These charts are also color-coded; you can see with just a glance whether prices rose or fell for the given day.

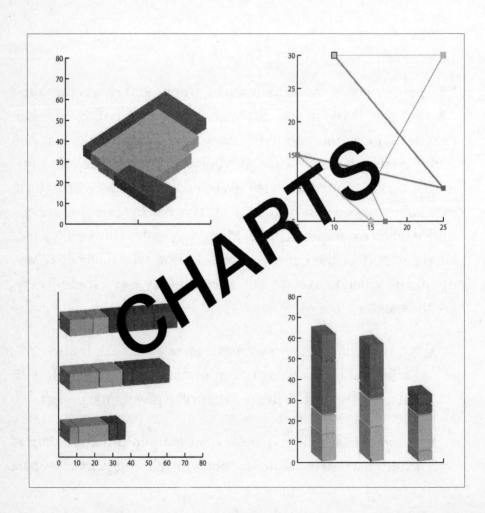

Line Charts

A line chart is composed of a single line over an x and y-axis, where price is the y-axis and date is the x-axis.

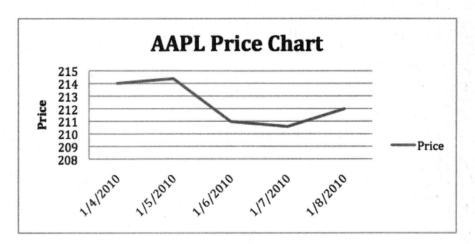

These charts are fairly easy to construct and even easier to read. The above chart for Apple, Inc. shows closing prices for the first week of 2010. As you can see, this type of chart alone leaves out quite a bit of information. Because the closing price is seen as the most important price when evaluating a stock, line charts typically will reflect that price, rather than opening, high, or low prices. This does not mean that line charts should be discounted, however. A line chart is the fastest way to evaluate a stock's progress over long periods of time. For the trader who looks at hundreds of charts each day, a line chart is a valuable tool because of the amount of time that is saved when using them.

Additionally, line charts are great for showing price changes over long periods of time because intraday changes are less important over the longer term. When it comes to intraday changes in price, line charts do not tell the whole story, though. More information is going to be needed for day traders.

Bar Charts

A bar chart contains more information than a line chart. The x- and y-axes are the same as in line charts, but more information is conveyed in the same amount of space. Take a look at the following bar chart of Apple Inc.

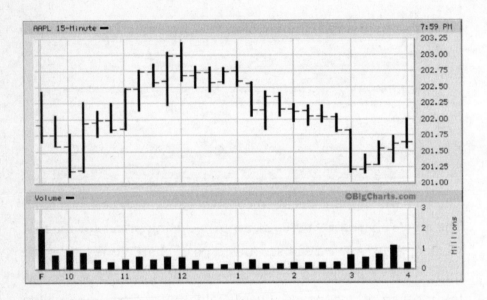

Again, this type of chart is not complicated. The body of each individual bar incorporates the high, the low, and every price in between for the given time period, in this case each 15-minute interval. The bar reflects the range of prices that a stock trades at over the given course of time with the day being the most commonly referenced unit. Take a closer look at one of the bars:

The opening price for the day on a bar is always the left line poking out from the main line, while the right protruding line is the closing price. As you can see, the above example started out low and eventually closed near its high for the day. The length of the bar indicates the amount of price change there was over the course of the day. The longer the bar, the higher the degree of volatility that occurred over the given time period. The body of the bar chart extends beyond the opening and closing prices in this example because the high for the day was higher than the closing price. The daily low was also lower than the opening price. This is common because rarely do stocks open or close at their exact high or low.

Bar charts are the most commonly referenced type of chart because they show all of the essential information when it comes to a stock's change in price over the course of time without being too complicated. Depending on what your intentions are and what kind of trading you are doing, this will be the type of stock chart you see most often.

Common bar chart indicators

There are many meaningful patterns that have emerged over the years that traders look at and try to decipher in bar charts. One of these is the head and shoulders pattern. This pattern is one of the more visible aspects of a chart. With a defined "head" surrounded by two "shoulders," the head and shoulder pattern signals a price reversal. When this pattern occurs at the top of an uptrend, a drop in price is more often than not about to happen. Look at a two-chart for Hasbro Inc. (HAS) on the following page to find a good example of a head and shoulders pattern. The three thin lines point to the left shoulder, the head, and the right shoulder, respectively. As you will see, the shoulders do not need to be the same shape or price. As long as the head is the most pronounced shape, this indicator need not be symmetrical.

For those short sellers that follow trends, the **inverse head and shoulders** is another pattern that should be acknowledged. This occurs at the bottom of a downtrend and is usually a signal that a bear trend has run its course. The inverse head and shoulders is a mirror image of the head and shoulders. Consider the following chart of the SPDR Dow Jones ETF (DIA).

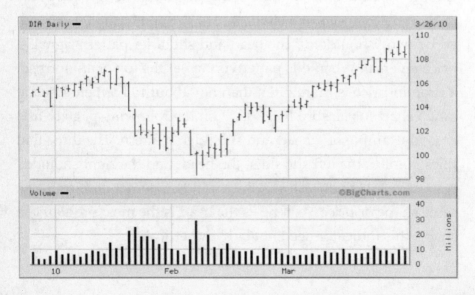

As you can see, shortly after the first week of February 2010, this ETF bottomed out at close to $98. Before that there had been a low of $100, followed by a very short-lived rally at the beginning of February. After the low of $98 though, there had been another rally up to just more than $104. This rally stalled out at $100, forming the second shoulder, before starting a rally that lasted the entire month of March.

If you were following this ETF as a short seller, your correct exit point would have been at $100. This might seem counterintuitive. Why would it not be at the lower price of $98? Ideally, this would be the optimum spot to exit the trade. But it is not realistic to time your trade exactly right. For technical analysts, there was no way to know that this ETF had reached its low. Instead, as a technical analyst, you need some sort of signal that the stock is done with its plummet. The stalling at $100 provided just this symbol.

The **inverted cup with handle** is a variation of the head and shoulders pattern. Rather than three highs, the inverse cup and handle consists of two highs, the first being broader and higher than the second. This is an indicator that the current high prices cannot be sustained; the second smaller "rally" confirms this.

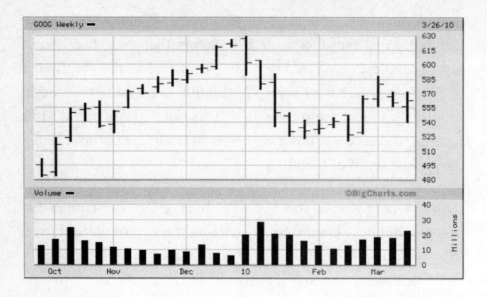

Look at the above chart for Google Inc (GOOG). At the beginning of January 2010, the stock had reached a high of $630 only to be down to $525 by February. The beginning of March saw a brief rally up to $585. It now appears that the stock has begun to once again decline. This is a classic example of the inverted cup with handle. Although this is a strong signal for the beginning of a short sale, only time will tell if it is a true signal.

Consolidation patterns are, by definition, almost non-patterns. This will occur when a stock appears to be moving sideways. There should be no major ups or downs, and the stock will be trading in a very tight formation. Usually, this is an indicator that traders are indecisive regarding a stock. These stocks will usually have a low trading volume. The chart on the next page shows a brief moment of consolidation within J. Crew Group's (JCG) stock. As you can see within the boxed area, the price fluctuated only slightly prior to dropping in price. Consolidation does not always indicate a drop in price; it sometimes will lead to rising prices or to no change at all.

A **gap down** is a divergence between two indicators on a chart. This can be caused by a sudden overnight change in trader sentiment regarding a stock or an abrupt turnaround in a stock's fiscal health. As you can see on the boxed section of the chart on the following page for Boyd Gaming Corp. (BYD), there is a slight gap down followed by a decline in price. The problem with a gap down pattern is that they are usually only apparent after the fact. Solely looking at a price chart will never predict a gap. Although by this reasoning gaps might appear to be anomalies, they occur quite frequently. Learning how to predict them can be quite profitable to a short seller because of the sudden and drastic drop in a stock's price. Some of the warning signs of a gap down can be a poor earnings report, newly reported shortcomings in a business's fundamentals, and other bad news for the company. In other words, it pays to examine both fundamental and technical indicators.

A **double top** is another pattern that can be advantageous to a short seller. Double tops flirt with a level of resistance twice before a final significant drop in price. For the chart on the next page of ATP Oil & Gas Corp. (ATPG), the level of resistance appears to be about $20.50. The boxed area shows the double top that is followed by a significant selling off of shares over the next several weeks. Volume is an important aspect of the double top. If the stock is churning, rising in price while volume stagnates, a price reversal becomes much more likely. This is the case for ATP Oil.

Candlestick Charts

Candlestick charting operates under the assumption that markets are partially determined by psychology. Originally invented in order to track the price of rice in Japan, candlestick charting is still relevant today because it packs a large amount of information into a tiny space; it combines the fundamentals of the line and bar chart into one. Take a look at what a typical candlestick configuration would look like:

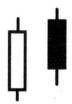 As you can see, individual candlesticks come in two varieties: black or white, with the shade of coloring depending on the specific broker or charting package you are using. White bodies indicate that the stock rose for the given time period while the black bodies mean the price dropped. The lines protruding from the top and bottom of the bar, the "wicks," indicate the high and

low prices for the given time. The main body of each candlestick bar represents the range that the stock traded in for the greatest portion of the day. The stock's opening and closing prices are determined by the outer limits of the candlestick's body. In a blank candlestick, the bottom portion is the opening and the top is the closing price; it is the other way around in a colored candlestick. The opening price is the top and the closing is the bottom. This multitude of information allows candlestick charts to take into account trader psychology, emotion, and sentiment.

Some people may wonder what psychology has to do with the price of a company's stock. Certainly, this is a valid concern; at first look it seems that consumer psychology plays only a little role within the daily fluctuations in price. But do not be fooled: Psychology plays a large role, especially for technical analysts. When you look at a price chart, you are not taking into account any of a company's inner-workings. Furthermore, each technical analyst is acting off of the same basic data: how a stock has performed in the past. And each technician is trying to guess what is coming next for the stock in question. In this light, psychology plays a huge role. The better you know how others will react to past changes, the better equipped you will be to predict future movement.

The Japanese traders that invented the candlestick charting method saw patterns repeating over and over again. These patterns still apply to today's stock market. Many of these patterns are effective because they are supposed to be. This sort of self-fulfilling prophecy works because it worked in the past. Now that more and more traders are wary of these signals, more people act upon them, causing the expected action of the stock's price to occur.

Below is a candlestick chart for Apple Inc. This chart shows the same time period with the same intervals that was used in the bar chart example earlier this chapter. Notice the different shading of the candlesticks. It is much easier to look at this chart and know what is going on right away than it was for the bar chart.

Because candlestick charts operate on the fact that the entities executing trades are living, breathing people, market psychology, as previously discussed, plays a large role in determining when to enter and exit a position. There are many different candlestick formations that give buy or sell signals and listing them all would take up a whole book in itself. Instead, this book lists the most pertinent ones to short sellers.

Chapter 7

Entry Strategies

K nowing when to enter a trade is one of the most written about aspects of trading. It is also one of the few things that you have complete and total control over when it comes to playing the market. Once the trade has been initiated, once that trigger has been pulled, your degree of control significantly diminishes. You cannot manipulate the market to your own liking; you can only hope to anticipate its moves. While no one can predict market movement 100 percent of the time, you can exert control on your end by entering at almost precisely the moment you wish to. The use of limit orders will greatly help to accomplish this.

There is no one strategy that will bring fantastic results. You must adapt and create your own strategy that works for you. There are many technical and fundamental indicators that give off selling signals; some of the most widely used indicators will also be covered in this chapter.

Regardless of which camp you are in, it is a good idea to be knowledgeable of the other methodology. When you are able to confirm an entry point with technical analysis and then double-check it with fundamental analysis, your odds of having a good and profitable trade improve drastically. If, on the other hand, there is a contradiction found, you can abandon the trade and return to it at a later time when the contradiction has gone away. There is no harm in abandoning a trade; this happens to even the best traders. Luckily for us the market is massive enough to supply us with more opportunities than we can handle. We just need to look carefully for them.

Your charting package will come with dozens of built in technical analysis methods, each with its own set of merits. In fact, there are far too many of these methods to discuss within the scope of this book, but discussed below are some of the indicators that analysts have deemed to be the most helpful.

The beauty of technical analysis is its quickness. There are no complicated formulas to worry about; the computer takes care of all these things for us. There is also no need to compare the collected data to other companies. Each chart is a standalone snapshot of a company. Furthermore, you can use technical analysis on anything including stocks, commodities, and currencies.

Technical analysis is limited though. It relies on the past to predict the future. While it can be argued that past prices and current consumer attitudes can dictate future prices, it does not change the fact that fundamental analysis is a far more exacting method. Whereas technicians have the ability to focus on several companies within the course of the day, fundamental analysts cannot move beyond the scope of a few different companies.

Moving Averages

As previously stated, a moving average is a technical indicator that measures a stock's change in price over a given time period. There are several indicators that use moving averages to operate, and some of the more useful ones are listed below. As with any indicator, these are not 100 percent accurate. Still, you should have confidence in your target prices and operate in a manner that betrays no fear.

Simple Moving Averages

Simple moving averages (SMA) weigh each unit of time the same. In the chart for Yahoo! (YHOO) on the next page, you can see that when the SMA for the shorter time period, the SMA (9), crosses to go below the longer time period, the SMA (18), prices tend to drop. This can be seen at about 1:20 p.m. and 3:20 p.m.

Exponential Moving Averages

SMAs are usually reliable signals, but they oftentimes occur too late to do anything about it. An exponential moving average (EMA), on the other hand, paints a much different picture. The EMA lines are much more finicky because they weigh current prices much more heavily than the past. Because of this, EMA lines tend to mirror prices more accurately. It is when prices rise above the EMA lines that they get poised to drop. You can see in the Yahoo! EMA chart on the following page that this occurs at about 12:20 p.m. and 2:30 p.m.

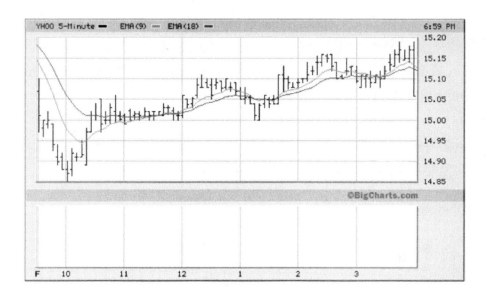

Price Channels

A price channel, much like a moving average, helps you see when a stock has become overbought or oversold. An overbought stock is a good candidate for initiating a short trade since a price correction is probably right around the corner. Price channels are largely arbitrary, but a good channel will enclose the vast majority of prices within the given stock. Software packages sometimes create channel lines with a formula that takes into account both exponential moving averages and a channel coefficient. Price channels tend to work much better than simple moving averages when a stock is trending because simple and exponential moving averages tend to lag several units of time behind the actual price. Exponential moving averages are, however, a bit more accurate during trends because they weigh current prices more heavily. Take a look at the one-day chart for Apple (AAPL). The price channel contains the vast majority of prices that the stock experienced during the course of the day. At around 12:15 p.m.,

Apple hit its high price by breaking outside of the price channel and then corrected itself by falling in price. The price once again broke through the upper channel line at around 2:20 p.m., only to slightly fall and then stall out for the rest of the day. As you can see, when a stock diverges from its channel, it usually is a precursor to a price reversal. This means that when a stock nears the bottom of the channel line, the trade should be covered.

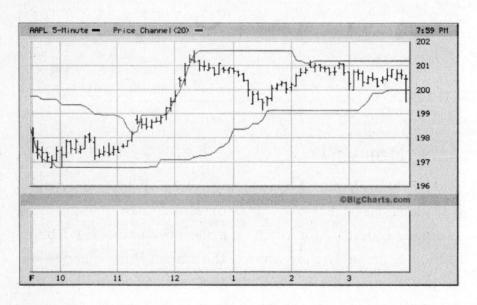

MACD

The Moving Average Convergence/Divergence indicator takes into account the 26-day EMA, the 12-day EMA, and a 9-day signal line, which is plotted on top of the MACD chart. The greater the degree of divergence, the more likely a price reversal is to occur. Another factor to take into account is when the MACD line pulls away from the signal line. These two lines cannot get too far away from each other since they both contain some bits of the same data. The farther away these two lines are, the more imminent a price reversal is. The histogram plotted on the centerline signifies the divergence in between price and the MACD line. When there is a large divergence between these two lines, it symbolizes the end of a trend. When there is a sizeable positive divergence, it is a strong indicator that prices are about to drop, making the stock attractive to short sellers.

The MACD charted below is Apple's one-day chart. As you can see, when the MACD line crosses the EMA line about 12:45 p.m., a price drop has just begun. MACD charts also measure the rate of divergence between the two lines. At the end of the day there was very little divergence in the price, indicating the trend will continue for at least the time being.

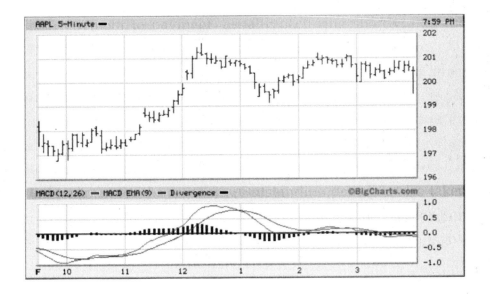

Resistance Levels

The resistance level is a range of prices that a stock just does not seem to be able to break out of. Support and resistance levels are not concrete. There is no mathematical formula for determining them. Instead, they are a range of prices loosely agreed upon by the trading public — remember trading psychology? Think of the support level as that on which the stock rests on, or what supports the price. The resistance level is the level at which the stock cannot break above, or the level at which it shows to be resisting. Only rarely does the stock break out of the upper resistance level, and when it does, a drop in price occurs directly afterward. The upper resistance level signifies a price that the trading public agrees is too high for the stock in question. Until something changes within the fundamentals of the stock, or something changes with the public's opinion of that stock, prices will rarely rise above the upper resistance level. The longer a stock sits at a resistance level, the more powerful of an indicator it is.

Look at the chart for the pharmaceutical company Pfizer Inc. (PFE) on the next page. The resistance and support levels for this stock are between $18 and $17.60. On the long side of things, we see that PFE sits at a support level just above $17.60 for almost all of Wednesday. When Thursday comes, it is still at that level, only to shoot up to $18. Come Friday it goes back to the $17.60 but only to slightly rise again. This can be an indicator that this stock's price is ready to rise, so short selling this particular stock at this time is not a good idea.

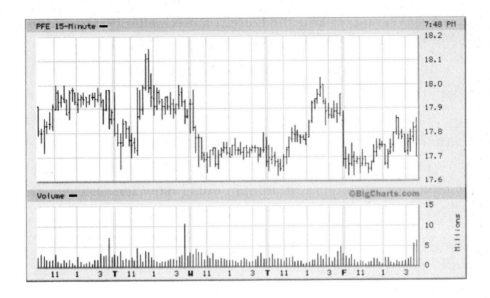

Railroad Tracks

When the railroad track pattern occurs, a pronounced downtrend is extremely likely to occur. This pattern is called "railroad tracks" because the parallel price lines on the chart look just like a pair of railroad tracks. This pattern will occur at or near the top of a price chart, sometimes there will even be a gap down following them. When stock prices repeatedly trace recent past performances, it is often an indicator of trouble to occur.

As you can see by the above chart, Berkshire Hathaway Inc. saw a railroad track pattern at the top of its daily chart. Shortly after, there was a pronounced gap down. This was followed by a small rally, and then a drop and a leveling off in price, where it remained for the rest of the day.

Overhead Supply

When a stock has reached new highs, it can be tempting to sell it short with the anticipation that it will soon drop in price. However, this can be a long and drawn out process. It is not until an overhead supply is established that you should enter a trade. This is defined as when a stock is trading at an extreme high, only to come down soon after. When the stock's rallies cannot break into the range that it was trading at just a short time ago, an overhead supply is said to exist. The head and shoulders pattern previously mentioned is a variation of the overhead supply pattern. Take a look at the chart below for Green Mountain Coffee Roasters to get an idea of what effect overhead supply has on the price of a stock:

This chart shows a double top, another variation of the overhead supply, followed by a sharp selling off of the stock.

Bearish Candlestick Indicators

Candlestick charts, because of their increased usefulness, often-times can show a set of signals to buy or sell a stock with just a few units of time measured. Some of the more useful of these distinct patterns are explained below. While these signals are not always 100 percent accurate, they are correct often enough to be profitable to the trader who practices strict money management skills.

 The **bearish engulfing pattern** occurs when the second unit of time measured covers a much wider array of prices with opening and closing prices much different from the previous day's, even going so far as to include a higher high than the previous unit. But the important piece is that on the second day, the stock ended far below its opening price. Usually this occurs when there is an increase in volume but the trading sentiment has begun to reverse itself. This pattern can be taken as a signal to initiate a short sale. A bearish engulfing pattern occurs when the following candlesticks are found together *(pictured to the left)*.

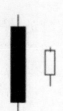 A **bearish harami pattern** shows that stock prices may have begun to increase, but they have not surpassed the previous high point. This can be a sign of a false rally. Time has shown us that the smaller the second candlestick is, the more pronounced the following downtrend will be. Rather than trying to time the initiation of a trade at the very top of the chart, this pattern takes into account the fact that markets will oftentimes trace back to where they were at a previous high point before falling. The bearish harami, unlike some other indicators, takes this into account. A bearish harami occurs with the following pattern *(pictured to the left)*.

 Closely related to the bearish harami is the **harami cross**. This pattern is an even stronger signal that a price trend is about to come to a reversal. The bearish harami cross signifies that an upward trend is coming to a halt. It is signified by a large period of increasing price followed by a bearish doji; a day of closely

bound prices that ends slightly down for the day. The pattern for a bearish harami looks like the following *(pictured to the left, page 162)*.

The **dark cloud cover** pattern shows that the first day of trading was a positive one for the stock in question. It ended the trading session with a large gain, only to see an even higher opening trade the following day. The second day sees a large drop in price, thus indicating that the stock's price has even further to fall in the near future. A dark cloud cover pattern resembles the following candlesticks *(pictured to the left)*.

The **hanging man** is one of the more famous of the candlestick patterns because of its distinct look and commonality. When the hanging man occurs at or near the top of a price chart, it oftentimes signals that the price is about to drop. Essentially, what the hanging man shows is a very tight trading range that contains a sudden and extreme low, yet recovers to end only slightly down for the session. A hanging man pattern looks like this *(pictured to the left)*.

The **kicker** is another bearish signal that will occur at the top of an uptrend. With a large gap down in between the positive and the negative trading sessions, the kicker reflects a sudden divergence in between price and trader sentiment. The kicker pattern shows an uptick in trading followed by a pronounced gapped downtick, as you can see in the below example *(pictured to the left)*.

The **gravestone doji** indicates price reversals at the end of a bullish trend. With the gravestone doji, the opening and closing prices for the day should either be identical or extremely close. When this symbol appears at the top of a bull trend, it can signify that prices are about to drop, thus making a short sale profitable. This is partially what gives the gravestone doji its name: it means the death of the current trend. Because there is a pronounced high point in the gravestone doji, it can be assumed that trading for the day was at a moderate to high volume, yet despite the exaggerated high price, consumer sentiment slipped at some point during the trading session. The opening and closing prices within a gravestone doji candlestick will be toward the low end for the day. This can been identified by the following pattern *(pictured to the left)*.

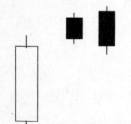

The aptly named **two crows** indicator shows us that a bearish reversal is about to occur. The two candlesticks with the black coloring look like crows flying overhead the other, positive candlestick. While the two crow candlesticks appear to be trading at higher prices, they both end down for the day. The gap up between the first and the second candlestick in this instance will usually be short-lived as stock prices prepare to tumble after the two crows. If the third trading session is engulfing the second session, as in the pattern, the signal that a drop in price is about to occur becomes stronger because of the false rally and the lower low *(pictured to the left)*.

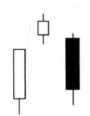

The **evening star** tells us that a bull trend has run its course. This pattern consists of a day that ended on the upward side, followed by a day that opened even higher and then closed up for the day. This second day needs to have a very tight trading range. However, the third day needs to open at around the same price only to fall drastically. The evening start pattern looks like the following *(pictured to the left)*.

Fundamental Indicators

So far, the entry strategies that we have discussed have used primarily technical analysis methods as indicators. Although it is impossible to fully master both types of indicators, a good grasp on both will only strengthen your ability as a trader. Technical analysis focuses on public sentiment and price, something that can translate across the board to any company or any commodity. With this type of trading strategy, you are setting your sights widely. Fundamental analysts, on the other hand, inhabit a niche of the market, focusing on a more narrow set of goals. These traders become experts in a certain type of trading, or a certain sector of the market. There is just too much information to take in to be effective with a fundamental trading strategy. Whatever the case may be, it is difficult for fundamental analysts to maneuver around the entirety of the market as easily as a technical analyst can. A technician can use his or her knowledge to trade commodities, options, and currencies just as easily as they trade shares of stock, but this does not make technical trading superior; some of the best traders in the world, such as Warren Buffett and Jim Cramer, are fundamental analysts. On the contrary, technical analysts are able to jump around to multiple marketplaces because they rely solely on the price of whatever it is they are trading and individuals' reaction to that price. Price charts and their patterns are universal; the price chart for Apple has the same major characteristics of a price chart for gold or the Yen.

Fundamental analysts do not have this luxury. Because they take a more in-depth analysis of the companies that they trade, they literally do not have the time to look at as many companies as technicians do. This does not make one style superior over the other; it is just as likely for a technician to succeed as a fundamental analyst.

Earnings reports and other financial documents

There is always a lot of activity when it comes time for a company to release its quarterly or yearly earnings report. There will usually be an increase in volume and sometimes a sudden jump or drop in the stock's price. There are even times when there is no change in price at all. Some traders swear by the release of earnings reports as a great way to anticipate a company's fiscal health. Others totally avoid trading a stock if an earnings report is scheduled in the near future because of the hoopla created.

If you must trade based on the release of an earnings reports, make sure you know exactly what you are looking for. By determining an underperforming company's **burn rate**, you can get a feel for how long a company can continue operating at the current pace. The burn rate is simply a figure that shows how long a company can spend before it is completely out of money, and therefore would need to declare bankruptcy. Of course, there are always exceptions to this; the company might be able to release a product that raises more money, or they may issue more shares of stock. Still, this will help you to determine which companies are in trouble. You can calculate the burn rate of a company with the following formula:

$$\frac{\text{Annualized negative cash flow}}{\text{Cash on hand as per balance sheet}}$$

If a company issues more shares of stock in a secondary offering, that company, no matter how poorly it had been performing, might see a sudden turnaround as its share increase in price as investors gobble up the new shares. A secondary offering is a generic term for any additional issuances of shares after the initial primary offering. Do not be fooled by this façade of profitability; if the company continues down the same fiscal path after the secondary offering, it might be a good candidate for a short sale further down the road. Secondary offerings are usually only patches for deeper running problem. While they may boost stock prices for a while, the windfall is usually short-lived. Chances are, the stock will continue its decline, only at a later date.

Past winners

It is usually the companies that benefitted the most from a bull market that are hit the hardest when the market turns bearish. Usually, this includes new companies that took advantage of heavy and unsustainable growth during the bull market buildup. Short sale candidates also include established companies that are selling new products or under new management. You can get this information from reading the business section of your newspaper or through online forums such as Yahoo! Finance (**http://finance. yahoo.com**) and The Motley Fool (**www.fool.com**).

This is simply the cycle that stocks prices run through. The economy expands and then contracts on a regular cycle. Many new companies will see unprecedented growth, only to come crashing down a few months later. Bubbles like this occur, on average, once or twice a decade. When bubbles pop and those companies that saw so much growth begin to correct their prices, a recession affecting the entire market will usually occur afterward. There are four main parts of a market cycle:

- **Peak**: When the economy is at its peak, it is performing at the highest level. Stock prices have been rising consistently and are at the highest point they could reach.

- **Downtrend**: Stock prices begin coming down and the nation's gross domestic product begins to suffer. Jobs might be lost as companies tighten their belts. After a few months of a downtrend, the economy is officially said to be in a recession. The downtrend is when short sellers should start to be excited. Stocks are tumbling down at this stage. The bottom of the market is still in the future.

- **Trough**: The trough occurs when the economy hits a bottom. Short sellers, if they are lucky enough to recognize the trough, should cover their positions. If a trough occurs for a long period of time, a depression will develop. The generally agreed upon timeframe for declaring a depression is when a trough occurs for six months or longer.

- **Uptrend**: When the economy begins to recover, stock prices will begin slowly rising. It takes much longer, in the vast majority of cases, for stocks to recover their prices than it does for them to come crashing down.

It is usually not until months after the fact that experts and analysts are able to definitely determine which period of the cycle the economy happens to be experiencing. By keeping your own tabs on how the economy seems to be functioning, you can stay one step ahead of the crowds.

It is important to keep tabs on the market cycles regardless, but this becomes especially important when considering those stocks that were most profitable during the uptrend and peak stages. These stocks may be poised to become even more profitable, this time to the short sellers.

Reverse splits

When a stock splits, whether it be because of an expanding product line, or the officers of the company just want to issue more shares, there is technically no change in the company's outstanding share value. A single share worth $100 would become two shares worth $50. This only occurs in theory, though. As you know, share prices are affected by consumer sentiment, not what the company says or thinks should happen. When a stock splits, the new shares are going to be priced at whatever the market conditions dictate.

The same holds true with reverse splits, technically. When two shares of $50 are morphed into one share of $100, there is no theoretical change in the value of outstanding shares. But reverse splits do make a large difference. A company does not commit to a reverse split during times of prosperity; usually reverse splits are executed in order to artificially increase their share prices. Because this increases the price per share of a stock, at first glance, it is assumed to have a positive effect on the company's shares. However, this is an artificial propping up of price and can sometimes signal a company's fiscal weakness.

An updated list of companies preparing to execute splits or reverse splits can be found at Yahoo! (**http://biz.yahoo.com/c/s. html**). This information can be very valuable to a short seller. If a company is consolidating shares, it is often a sign that prices are on their way down. By knowing ahead of time when a split or reverse split is approaching, you give yourself a large advantage over the masses.

When a stock is range-bound

If you wish to day trade, it is possible to make money off of almost any stock, even one that has become range-bound, which is when a stock is trading within a tight range of prices. This is accomplished through good timing and large amounts of money. For example, if a particular stock is trading between $20 and $21 per share, you can enter a limit order for $21 for 1,000 shares. When the stock hits your cover point, you will buy back the shares. It is important that your buying price not be too low. If the stock for some reason breaks out of its range before reaching an extreme low, you could be in big trouble if you do not have a stop-loss point in place. It is because of this that stop-loss points should always be used, no matter how foolproof the trade looks to be. There is simply no such thing as a foolproof trade. In the above example, you would then set your cover point as a limit order for $20.50. This would give you a profit of $500 before fees and commissions. If this stock is fluctuating between these prices often, you might earn this amount in just a few hours. As in this example, a large amount of shares are necessary in order to make a profit. Day traders will sometimes trade 10,000 shares or more with a single trade just to avoid slippage costs.

Where to Look

You have many options concerning where to look for potential trades, but they basically boil down into four main groups:

- Search throughout the entire market.
- Search throughout a niche sector of the market.
- Pay someone to search the market for you.
- Join a group that collectively shares stock picks.

1. Searching the market

The market is a vast and scary place for the new short seller. With so many stocks to choose from, how can you possibly look at each and every company? To put it quite simply: You cannot. There are just too many publicly traded companies out there for you to possibly examine them all.

If you want to scour the market, looking for that perfect trade wherever it might be hiding, you will have to use some of the tools at your disposal. Newspapers, such as the *Investor's Business Daily,* will oftentimes highlight several stocks that stick out as prominent candidates, both for long and short trades. You can also refine your search with resources such as Web sites and software packages. The more you read, the more widespread your knowledge will be. If you are truly passionate about finding the right trades, this will be an enjoyable experience.

2. Searching a sector

By narrowing your search to a particular sector of the market you are greatly improving your chances of success. Sectors tend to walk in lock step with each other, so you will not always be able to sell stocks short by using this method. When a sector is in an upward trend, most, if not all, of the stocks comprising the sector will act in accordance. Instead practicing a short sale, you will be partially limited to acting in a manner suitable to the market conditions of the time because of our old friend, oscillation.

Of course, your ability to short sell will be limited by the type of trading you are doing. A day trader will have no problem finding daily drops in price, but a swing or position trader will have a difficult, if not impossible, time short selling during a bull market. Company's move up and down, even if their overall trend is up. If you are a day trader, you will not be limited to a particular sector's trend. Instead, you will need to examine intraday charts and determine when a stock has reached its upward level of resistance. If a particular stock has broken through its resistance, day traders will oftentimes bank on the chance that it will come tumbling down soon afterward. You will want to choose a sector that you are knowledgeable of. If you are not an expert in the field you want to trade, become one. Study articles on the industry you choose. For example, a subscription to a medical journal may be worthwhile if you are interested in trading within the pharmaceutical industry. This would allow you to see which medications are being prescribed most often, and thus which companies are raking in the most profits.

3. Buying stock tips

There is no need to buy stock tips, which come from market pundits and others looking to make a quick buck. You have probably seen advertisements for these systems on the Internet. But with so many resources out there, why would you spend your money on something other than your own trade? There are no quick profit systems out there, regardless of what the system you see advertised touts. You need to do the work yourself because only you can determine which trades are best.

4. Join a group

There are many trading groups out there. You can find them on Facebook, Google Groups, or more locally through your own stockbroker or investment advisor. But just by joining a group, it does not mean that you do not need to work hard; there are very few easy things about trading. But a trading group allows you to bounce ideas around, gain another's perception, and test your trading theories. A trading group can keep you levelheaded during good times, and be your emotional support during bad times.

CASE STUDY:DAY TRADING

Keith McHugh is a day trader. With Goldman Sachs as his primary brokerage, McHugh spends his day dealing mostly in stocks and exchange-traded funds and aims to make about $10,000 per month. By focusing on 10–15 different stocks per day, he focuses on an equity's momentum when making decisions. Each night after the markets close, he looks through his charts searching for patterns that will pay out the following day. When it comes time to act, his activity depends on how fast or slow the market is moving. Like many other traders, McHugh will not fight against a stock's trend. Whether he is long or short on the trade largely will depend on the momentum that stock is seeing.

McHugh agrees that a trader needs to be disciplined. "In my experience traders are mentally tough," he said. And because the market is always changing, McHugh argues that successful traders need to be willing to change too, something that takes quite a bit of self-education. By reading newspapers such as the Wall Street Journal and the Investor's Business Daily, McHugh attempts to accomplish this. He also is a regular reader of trading strategy blogs.

Losses are occasional but inevitable. By taking regular breaks and getting away from his computer screen a few times a day, McHugh gives himself the opportunity to regroup his thoughts. By giving his emotions a break once in a while, McHugh returns to his day refreshed and ready.

Common Mistakes

There are several instances when you will want to avoid shorting stocks. One of these is when a stock continuously hits new highs. Yes, it may have previously been a range-bound stock, stagnating around the same price for several days. But by no means does this mean that the stock continues to be range bound. As you may have noticed, market tops are much more exaggerated than market bottoms. Highs tend to last longer than lows because market sentiment is different at the top than it is at the bottom. As more and more people try to join the party at the top of the price line, there is often a secondary wave of demand for the stock, forcing prices to stay high for longer than they naturally would. While market bottoms tend to be built on fear, the top is built on greed, and people are much more likely to hold onto their greed. Greed is a more pleasant feeling than fear, and because of this, it sometimes goes unrecognized. By being aware of these emotions, you will be minimizing the magnitude of poor trading decisions.

Another mistake is shorting with too much at risk. Because tops tend to last longer than bottoms, it is inevitable that you are going to occasionally get trades wrong the first time. When a trade hits its stop-loss point, this does not necessarily mean that you should abandon the trade. If you have carelessly used up all of your capital allocated for a particular trade, the trade will be over for you. But if you have not hit your maximum allocation, you can cover your position when the price hits your stop and then open up a new short sale. This will not always be a realistic choice for you because sometimes you will realize that you were wrong in your original choice to short the stock at that price. However, if you remain confident in your decision and you are disciplined, this might be a good option for you.

Another thing the more conservative short sellers will want to avoid is the trading of stocks that are very rarely traded. The brokerage you work with may need to end your trade early if you borrow a large portion of shares of which they only have a few. Remember, margin accounts do not have precedent over cash accounts. If another trader wishes to sell the shares that you have borrowed from them, your position will end early, regardless of whether the trade was profitable for you or not.

Chapter 8
Other Types of Short Selling

Traditionally short selling a stock can be an extremely rewarding and profitable practice, but it is not the only way to make money on the short side of a trade. There are several different types of short selling that you may wish to partake in either to add variety to your portfolio or to find a type of trading that you are even better at. Up until now, we have solely discussed the traditional short sale, where a stock is borrowed, sold, and then bought at a lower price before it is returned. This is short selling in its purist form, but it is not the only type of short sale that is possible. Some of the most popular variations of the short sell involve inverse Exchange Traded Funds, hedge funds, commodity futures, the forex market, and put options.

Naked Shorts

Naked shorts are an illegal form of the traditional short sale. These trades are called naked shorts because there is no protection for the trader committing the transaction. A naked short occurs when shares of stock are borrowed and sold without those shares actually being possessed by the person trading them. This can easily occur if your broker does not check to make sure that the proposed shares are possessed in another trader's margin account. Generally speaking, when a trader wishes to short a particular stock, their broker must have those specific shares available or be able to obtain them by borrowing from another broker for the trader. Naked shorting does not usually occur with a malicious intent to break the law. This type of trading is generally committed accidentally and is sometimes not even apparent that it has occurred until long after the trade has been finalized. Because short sales are usually shorter lived than long sales, this act has been a problem in the past. Before a broker is even able to recognize that a naked short has taken place, the trade is over. In theory, a naked short allows a trader to make money without shares of stock ever changing hands.

It should be noted that the main perpetrators of naked shorts are brokers. If they hurry through a trade without making the necessary searches through margin accounts, it is easy for them to overlook these illegal short sales. This is what gave birth to Regulation SHO.

Regulation SHO

Regulation SHO was signed into law in 2005 and prohibits naked short sales. There are two parts to this regulation: the locate and the close out. Locate refers to the broker's ability to actually possess the shares that are to be borrowed for a short sale, and close out refers to the increased need to actually deliver the shares that are to be shorted. The main purpose of this law is to prevent unethical short selling.

Regulation SHO was amended in 2007 with the caveat that brokers publish lists of stocks that frequently fail to deliver. If the stock you are trying to short happens to be on this list, your broker may nullify the trade before they execute it for you.

Goldman Sachs is a prime example of the repercussions this law poses. The financial company was accused of trading with naked shorts between 2008 and 2009, right after the government began cracking down more strictly on the practice. Although the company did not admit to any wrongdoing immediately, they paid $450,000 as a settlement.

Just because naked short sales of stock are illegal, it does not mean that this strategy cannot be used with other types of trading. The forex market is generally free of regulation, and naked short sales are generally a regular occurrence.

Foreign Exchange

The forex market is the world's biggest marketplace. Every day, trillions of dollars are exchanged between the people of different countries. Some do this out of necessity, whether it be travel or international business, while others trade currencies to make a profit. However, currency is difficult to trade because the markets move 24 hours per day. With the stock market, you have only a few given hours that you need to pay attention because the Wall Street stock markets are open only from 9:30 a.m. to 4 p.m. (EST). Within the currency market, because it is a global business, prices are always moving, even when you are sleeping. It is because of this constant momentum that it is very important to have stop and limit orders in place in case the markets change for the worst while you are not monitoring them.

Selling a currency short is different than selling a stock short. For one, currencies are linked to other currencies, rather than a security such as shares of a stock. When you sell a currency short, in essence, what you are doing is selling one currency and buying another. This makes currency short sales almost identical to going long with a stock. Each and every trade within the forex market is long on one currency and short on another.

There are a few different classes of investors and traders that use the forex market, including banks, brokers, and individuals. Banks, both private and federal, make up a very large proportion of forex traders. With so many banks involved in the market, it is often hard for the little guy to make money. For instance, an individual money manager may wish to convert $1 million into Japanese Yen. The bank that the investor goes through may front the 90 million Yen to the money manager, although it may not actually conduct the trade. The bank would then wait until the Yen is at an even better deal and purchase 100 million Yen. This involves a degree of speculation, but for banks, this is a regular moneymaking practice. If this were to happen with a stock exchange it would be considered illegal, but because the forex market is largely unregulated, this practice is allowable.

The forex market remains unregulated out of necessity. It is virtually impossible for there to be a central regulatory body because of its vast size and scope. Because many trades occur between brokers and banks making deals with other brokers and banks, the majority of trades occur in the private realm. It would be impossible for a governing body to regulate each and every trade.

Besides consumer psychology, there are several factors that influence currency prices, and gross national product (GNP) is one of the most important of these factors. The amount of money that a company earns is a good indication of that nation's overall fiscal health; it also is an indicator of how active the nation's cash flow is, both domestically and in the foreign markets. If a country has a high gross national product, the country is probably actively selling goods all around the world. A country's national debt is also a strong economic indicator. If a country is unable to pay their bills in a timely manner, their currency will usually drop in value. In other words: the stronger the economy, the stronger the currency. Take the nation of Greece, for example. They have recently experienced a crisis as their country nears default on loans from their creditors and other nations. As a result, the Greek economy and currency have gone through a dramatic drop in value.

Another key factor is the political sentiment within a country. If a country is going through political turmoil or a civil war, their currency will normally drop in value on the worldwide market. Besides political activity, the type of government also plays a role in forex pricing. The currencies of democracies tend to have higher relative values than other nations. This is apparent through the volumes of currency traded. The four most popular currencies to trade all come from major democratic powers: the U.S. dollar, the European Union's euro, the Japanese yen, and Great Britain's pound.

If you are interested in trading within the forex marketplace, strongly consider paper trading first. Many forex sites, such as FX Solutions (**www.fxsolutions.com**), will help you set up an account and then make trades with fake money until you have gained enough expertise to begin trading real money.

The forex market remains largely unregulated to this day. Whereas with margin accounts, you have 1:1 leverage, some forex clearinghouses will supply you with up to 400:1 leverage, giving you the purchasing power of 400 times the amount you actually are using to trade. With this type of purchasing power, each dollar you invest can purchase $400 worth of another currency. The odds are stacked against the naïve trader in this instance. While there is great potential for gains because of the lack of foreign and domestic regulations regarding the forex market, there is an even greater chance that your trades will be losing ones. The more knowledgeable you are though, the better your chances of success. This book is designed to get you to the next level with your trading.

The **forex futures** market is a different story. This type of trading is much safer for consumers in that it does not allow as much leverage as a straight currency exchange would allow you to. Although the potential benefits of a regular forex transaction are much higher than within the futures market, it is only potentially so. You are not guaranteed any profits in the forex market, and if the currency you are betting on plunges south, your risk factor skyrockets. With forex futures, you are required to put more money in your account than you would need to for a regular forex transaction. So, futures give you a degree of safety in that your potential for loss is limited.

According to some analysts, the forex market is not designed for swing traders. When you buy currencies, you should either do so as a day trader or as an investor. This is because the forex market never sleeps. Unless you are constantly at your computer, the majority of trades occur while you are not paying attention. This drastically increases the need to have stop-loss points firmly in order. Because currencies tend to fall into a trend more often than not, they are not meant as trades for an intermediate term. Major currencies will experience ups and downs just as any financial product will on a daily basis, but they tend to stay within a tight range and seldom stray outside of the current trend they are experiencing.

CASE STUDY:
A DAY IN THE LIFE OF A
CURRENCY TRADER

Randy Mowers wakes up each day before 4 a.m. It is necessary for him to wake up so early because Mowers manages a hedge fund that relies primarily on the trading of currencies. The forex market is truly a global marketplace, and Mowers takes full advantage of this. Trading currencies in Asia and Europe, as well as the U.S. dollar, is a daily ritual for him. An average day for his fund consists of 25 to 50 trades and millions of dollars.

A credible track record is necessary, along with obtaining the appropriate licenses, before an individual can begin trading with other people's money. Mowers has been a professional currency trader since 2006, first beginning to trade currency for his own profit in 2004. Over the years, he has successfully handled billions of dollars. With such high stakes, he stays focused on his results. Rather than trying to compare himself to a market benchmark, Mowers focuses solely on absolute returns, only measuring his success by how much money has made for his clientele.

Mowers contends that he needs to "stay humble and be a realist" in order to survive the natural ups and downs of the market. It is his discipline that makes him a successful trader though. When it comes to advice for other traders, Mowers stresses this discipline: "Never ever enter into an order without the appropriate protections." Stop-loss points are especially important in the forex market since you are dealing with a much higher degree of leverage.

Mowers is a supporter of naked short selling. Although this practice is illegal when it comes to short selling a stock, it is a common practice in other markets. Although this can be dangerous, if approached with a degree of caution, the short seller can make a huge profit. By selling a currency that is not owned, you can net a large profit without actually owning the currency that you are trading.

Shorting a Nation's Market

There is an alternative to currency trading if you do not want to venture into the risky world of forex. This involves shorting an entire foreign market, or rather, a particular nation's prominent stock exchange. This also carries with it a degree of risk, but with the proper techniques, you can drastically reduce this level of risk.

Just as you would trade an index fund, such as the S&P 500 domestically, shorting a foreign market usually involves short selling an index fund for the specific exchange. Another technique is to trade inverse ETFs that represent some or most of an entire nation's market. There are a number of factors that affect foreign markets, but they can be broken down into four main categories:

- The nation's bonds market.
- The value of the nation's currency.
- The gross national product.
- The effect of foreign investment dollars.

Bond markets

The bond market is a key factor in determining when to short a nation's markets because the bonds being issued largely reflect current market trends within a nation. This is the case for both government and corporate bonds. For example, if the nation happens to be struggling to raise capital, it may have recently raised its government bond rates in order to attract more capital. This in turn would mean that companies would have to raise bond rates in order to stay competitive. By being aware of a nation's bond market, you will have your finger on the pulse of that nation's metaphorical heartbeat.

Bond rates go up and down, but your foreign trades should reflect the momentum of the nation's bonds. If government bond rates are increasing in an effort to attract capital because of a dire national budgetary need, you need to be aware of the reasoning behind this increase. Are national companies struggling? Is the nation in danger of defaulting on loans from other countries? Without fully answering questions of this nature, you are entering the trade blindly and thus taking a gamble.

Currency

If the bond market is the heartbeat of a nation, currency is the blood pumping through its veins. Your trades should also be a mirror image of the nation's currency price. When the dollar is strong in comparison to the currency of the nation in question, the weaker the foreign market's currency will be. This can further be extrapolated to imply that the nation's companies and stock exchanges will also be made weaker. When the advantage is in your hands because of a strong dollar, it is a smart move to short the nation's exchange.

You are not exactly trading in currency when you are shorting a nation's exchange venue. Rather, you are looking at exchange rates as a determining factor as to whether you should trade within a foreign nation's market. A knowledge of currency trading is extremely helpful, but you do not necessarily need to be a professional forex trader to succeed.

Gross national product

As discussed in the forex section, the overall economy of a nation will play a large part in determining how their particular companies and stock exchanges function. If a nation is experiencing a recession, the domestic companies' performances will likely suffer, making them prime candidates for a short sale. Given that the United States began its recession at the end of 2008, the vast majority of U.S. companies at this time could have been targeted by short sellers. Gross national product is a great way of showing how productive a nation's industries are. When measured against national debt, you can get a rough idea of the deficit or surplus that the nation is operating under.

Foreign investments

The inflow and outflow of foreign investment dollars is a bit more difficult to ascertain; investments from other nations by both institutional and individual investors are traceable though. By paying attention to what analysts and fund managers are doing, you can get a general idea of how many dollars are being pumped into a foreign nation's economy. Stay away from the wisdom of emerging market governments and fund managers who have a lot to lose. These are biased sources and need to be taken with a grain or two of salt.

An additional factor that sometimes will come into play is whether the government of a particular country is manipulating a nation's currency. This usually occurs in the emerging markets sector because emerging market nations are less likely to have profitable companies operating within their borders. This makes sense as emerging markets are labeled "emerging" because they are still growing. Governments are oftentimes forced to intervene within their economies in order to prevent company failures.

The major idea to take away from this is the fact that government manipulation creates bubbles within the market. When stocks or other financial instruments trade at an extremely inflated price, it is only a matter of time before the bubble bursts and the markets correct themselves. Bubbles have occurred in our own country; consider the dot-com bubble or the more recent housing bubble. These can have disastrous effects on an economy, but if you can spot them and time your entry correctly, there is much potential for successful short sales. Markets tend to fluctuate toward their most efficient price; a government can only prop up their economy for so long before the true price of their markets emerges.

Types of foreign markets

There are two types of nations that are included in this broader topic: developed and emerging markets. With each of these categories comes their own set of things to look out for. The first step is to see if your broker even trades with stocks from the country you are interested in. If you are trading with a larger brokerage and you are looking at trading within developed nations, this will probably not be a problem. If you have trouble accessing the shares that you wish to short, your best bet is to open an account with a brokerage within the given nation. This will most likely be the case if you are planning on trading with a more remote emerging marketplace because many brokerage houses within the United States do not have access to these companies.

Developed nations

Besides traditional long and short trades, the vast majority of stock exchanges within the developed world allow for options and ETFs to be bought and sold over their particular stock exchanges. Examples of these markets include the FTSE 100 within Great Britain, the CAC 40 in France, and the German DAX 30. These are their respective countries' equivalent of the Dow Jones Industrial Average. In light of this, put options and inverse ETFs are also tradable within these major nations' economies, although they do not see the same type of liquidity that their U.S. counterparts experience. Basket funds that attempt to mimic major foreign indices are available through most domestic brokerages. These ETFs and mutual funds are not mirror images, though; if your target domestic fund diverges from the target foreign index, you may be in for a nasty surprise. While the target economy may be declining, your fund may not be 100 percent in sync with the drop in price. Because of this, you need to pay attention to the prospectus for any domestic fund claiming to be based off of foreign stocks or indices. Major divergences within such a fund might be indicators of problems within that domestic fund.

Emerging nations

For most emerging nations, it will be difficult to find consistent liquidity of specialized trades like put options. However, the liquidity of inverse ETFs should not prove to be a problem since they are actually domestic funds. ETFs, however, are not exact mirror images of the index they are supposed to be tracking. As stated above knowing how these funds diverge from the original is extremely important.

It should also be acknowledged that political events within smaller nations would have a more profound effect on the companies and therefore the markets within that nation. In reality, these nations are the ones most often in turmoil to begin with. Knowing exactly how an event will affect a nation's economy is hard to say; retrospection is sometimes the only way to judge an economy's status. However, if an event occurs that you think will adversely affect the nation's economy, you should wait for the technical indicators to affirm this prior to acting. A prime example of this is the 2010 debt crisis in Greece. When the nation announced that it was going to default on their loans without some sort of bailout, the world's markets plummeted. This was especially true within Europe. This would have been a great time for short-term traders to short European shares.

Technical analysis is probably the most effective way of looking at emerging markets because of the potential volatility within these markets. For major indices within these markets, the volume is not nearly the same as it would be in a developed nation's market. Therefore, they are more prone to the violent ups and downs that plague small-cap businesses within our own markets. Technical analysis is needed because fundamental analysis is too difficult for a little-known company. You will have better luck in this case looking at price charts and acting off of the universally recognized buy and sell signals that are highlighted in this book.

American Depository Receipts (ADR) can also be traded in representation for foreign companies. These products trade exactly like stocks, even to the point that some pay out dividends. ADRs are shares of foreign companies that trade domestically within the United States. This is not uncommon; rather than having NYSE or NASDAQ call signs as domestic companies within these markets possess, these companies trade on the U.S. market through their respective ADRs. ADRs must be issued by a U.S. bank; these can be bought for either a long position or sold short. ADR owners can trade their shares in for the actual share of the foreign company, but in most cases, this does not occur since they are more liquid as ADRs.

Inverse Exchange-traded Funds

Inverse ETFs act as an opposite of how an ETF would normally function. They are designed to act as if they held short positions in the index that they represent, thus making them a valuable investment during bear markets. While short selling is a principal method used in establishing inverse ETFs, the investment product does not act in the same way an actual short sale of the ETF normally would for the trader. For one, inverse ETFs do not expose traders to the same level of risk because these are not true short sales, and as such, they do not come with the risk of infinite losses. A trader who wishes to engage in this practice can only lose their principal investment. Another major difference is that inverse ETFs generally have slightly higher associated fees and costs simply due to the fact that they are typically more actively managed than their "long" counterparts. Because these basket funds involve short selling, options, and other active investing practices, they require a more hands-on style of management — with this comes a higher fee.

This does not necessarily mean that they will have higher payouts, though. Trading inverse ETFs is not as risky as shorting a stock, making this alternative a safer approach. Because ETFs generally have a much higher volume and a much larger amount of money flowing through them, they do not fluctuate as drastically as stock prices do. One thing to be aware of with inverse ETFs is that you do not actually sell them short. Rather than borrowing the shares and selling them first, inverse ETFs are designed to be treated like long positions. They are bought and sold in the traditional manner. They merely base their performance off of short positions held within their funds.

Hedge Funds

Although you cannot technically short a hedge fund, the fund manager will oftentimes use short positions within their fund. Because a hedge fund is designed to make money regardless of how the market performs, during bear markets, hedge funds use quite a bit of short positions so that they may profit from the falling stock prices. Hedge funds are primarily used to reduce the risk associated with traditional mutual funds. During bear markets, mutual funds that consist of solely long positions tend to decline in value. Although these funds minimize losses due to their diversified asset allocation, they do not hold short positions. This means that they will only do as well as the market itself is doing; this inevitably leads to a drop in price during bear markets.

Why, then, do more people not take advantage of hedge funds? Hedge funds are typically open only to a select group of investors. Because they are not public funds, hedge funds are exempt from many of the SEC regulations that govern other funds. The laws state that when there are fewer than 100 "qualified" investors in a fund, there is no need to comply with most of the regulations set forth for public investment companies.

Qualified Purchaser

According to SEC regulations, a 3(c)(7) fund must be comprised solely of qualified purchasers. The definition of a qualified purchaser is an individual with more than $5,000,000 in expendable assets.

Due to the lack of regulations, hedge funds are able to use other investment products usually banned from traditional public funds; options and leveraged trades are some of the more popular choices that investment professionals in the field will use. The forex market is a popular tool for many hedge fund managers because of the extremely inflated leverage rates available.

Hedge funds are not for the typical investor. The average trader does not have the means to take part in these types of funds because of the qualified purchaser requirement. Still, they may be an option for some.

Commodity Futures

Commodity futures first became popular amongst farmers looking to secure a fair and consistent price on their crops and other goods. By having a price guaranteed to them for several months down the road, these farmers were able to stop worrying about short-term price fluctuations in their harvest's value. Today, anyone can take advantage of commodity futures.

Commodities and commodity futures cannot be traded with your traditional brokerage. Instead, you must set up an account with a member of the exchange that you wish to trade within. This may sound like an inconvenience, but it is simply how these markets work. Rather than being monitored by the SEC, commodity futures are monitored by the Commodity Futures Trading Commission (CFTC), a division of the U.S. Department of Agriculture. Your average stock brokerage simply does not have the necessary licenses to conduct commodity futures trading because it is a completely different set of tests to pass and licenses to obtain.

When you enter a commodity futures position, you are solely entering a contract. Unlike when shares of stock are purchased, there is no ownership change at the time of signing of the contract; the binding contract just states that you will be either purchasing or selling the given commodity at a set price on the given date. A nominal margin deposit is required by both parties involved in order to make the contract valid. You do not need to worry about stockpiling these commodities in your home since the vast majority of futures are sold before they come to fruition. Instead, traders act as intermediaries between the producer of such goods and the end buyer. This helps to regulate market prices, and for many, it ends up earning them extra money.

There are two groups involved in the buying and selling of futures: hedgers and speculators. Hedgers include farmers and vendors for the commodity being traded while speculators include traders, including short sellers, looking to profit from, but not actually acquire, the commodity. Both groups are attempting to make a profit, although their styles differ dramatically. The hedgers, the parties most directly involved in the producing and distribution of the commodities, deal with the actual product. They enter futures contracts because they want a guaranteed price for their goods. They do not want a gamble.

Speculators, on the other hand, are in the futures market because of the gamble. These traders will never see the product that they are trading. Instead, the contract is what interests them. They are in the futures business for the sole reason of making money. These speculators will risk their money without possessing the offsetting asset. This results in either a pure monetary gain or a pure loss because they do not have anything else at stake.

There are natural highs and lows that commodities experience. Unlike stocks, commodities are tangible goods and because of this, there is only so much that a buyer will be willing to pay, and only so little that a seller is willing to part with. Prices will fluctuate between these highs and lows, with drops in price occurring much more quickly than rises. Supply and demand are the major dictators of futures pricing.

When it comes to commodity short selling, it is usually the professional fund managers that take part. This should be your first clue that there is money to be made here. Because price drops can occur quickly and unexpectedly, long positions can turn out to be very dangerous. This is why many of the professionals in the commodity futures market will hedge their bets with short positions. In effect, professionals are looking to profit on one end of the trade. If this does not look as if it will be profitable for the trader, they will seek to minimize losses on the other end. If these were not successful and profitable trading strategies year after year, the professionals would not consistently be trading in this manner. Because these professionals are in the market to make money, they do not short commodities just to merely protect their assets. They do so to make a profit, regardless of how poorly the market performs.

One strategy for profiting is known as straddling. This involves taking both a long and a short position simultaneously. It would be foolish to take a long and a short position for the same product under the same time constraints so the most common approach to avoid this is known as an intramarket spread. **Intramarket spreads** consist of a simultaneous long and a short position that expire at different times. For example, one might take a long position on corn for August, but short on corn for October when it is more plentiful and prices are more likely to drop. In theory, if the spread is large enough, the straddle will produce a gain regardless of what happens to the actual price of the commodity. This might not make sense at first. For example, imagine one were to buy two positions for crude oil: one long position expiring in September, and the other short position expiring in December. If the price has risen by September and the first trade is profitable, the trader can choose to sell their second contract early, thus losing only the cost of the contract.

There is a phenomenon that happens with futures contracts known as the basis, which is the difference in the cash value of the commodity being traded and the future price. A short seller will run into trouble here when the basis widens. When the cash price drops below the future price, the short seller will face a loss.

The act of shorting a commodity is a bit more intricate than the traditional short sale of a stock and it takes quite a bit of practice to master it. This type of trading is definitely not for everyone as a futures contract encompasses a good deal of time in comparison to a traditional short sale. Rather than holding a position for a few hours, days, or weeks, you will be holding the futures contract open for up to several months.

Short Selling Real Estate

The short sale of a piece of real estate is quite different than the short sale of a stock. With real estate, a short sale takes place when the selling price of the property is less than the amount owed by the mortgage holder. This is done in order to avoid a foreclosure action upon a property. All parties involved must agree to this procedure in order for it to take place, including the bank to which the mortgage is owed. All proceeds from the short sale are given to the bank in exchange for an end to the foreclosure process.

This may not seem like the best option, but it does present an interesting opportunity to the party named in the foreclosure. Because this ends the foreclosure process, a negative report on credit reports is avoided. Short sales are a type of settlement, and they do appear on credit reports, but they are much less detrimental than a foreclosure is.

Short selling can be mutually beneficial. Not only does it have a better impact on the debtor's credit report, it also saves the lender a good amount of legal fees. If it is determined that the legal fees subtracted from the minimum amount that the house would be auctioned for is smaller than the short sale amount, the lender can actually make money by approving the short sale. It is also a much quicker process, meaning that the lender would receive his or her money sooner.

On the buying end of things, short selling real estate can be a great opportunity for those looking to get a good deal on a piece of property. If you purchase a home at a discount because of a short sale, the opportunity for arbitrage presents itself. You can purchase the home, and then sell it at your convenience for the actual value of the home. This process is commonly known as "flipping" a house.

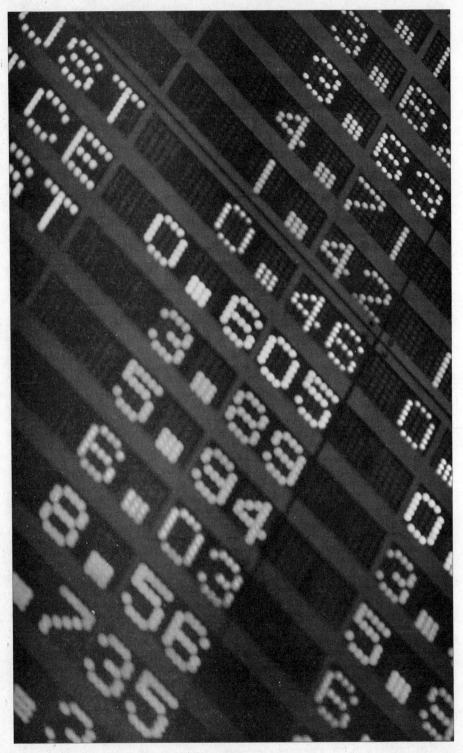

Chapter 9
Put Options

If you are still not convinced that short selling is a worthwhile supplement to your portfolio, this chapter is for you. Put options can be the safest version of the short sell because you do not actually have to enact the trade if prices do not change in the manner you wish them to. While Chapter 1 briefly talked about what an option was, here you will learn why put options are a vital part of your portfolio, regardless of whether you are a risk taker or a more conservative trader.

This is not to say that options are without risk. On the contrary, oftentimes you will be paying a fee for a trade that never pans out. Options are a wasting asset — they lose value as time goes by. In other words, you will be paying a hefty price for the luxury of time. Options will sometimes attract traders because they have the illusion of safety since there is no requirement that you actually have to follow through on your contract. For many traders, this safety is very real. But if you do not know what you are doing, these products can be very dangerous. Contract costs can be expensive, and the option will deteriorate in value quickly. The element of time is actually your biggest enemy; if your stock does not achieve the price you want it to quickly enough, your contract will expire and you will have lost the trade and your contract fee.

There are two main types of options: call and put. They both work quite similarly, except that the role of the trader is reversed. A call option is the equivalent of a long trade where a contract is made up and the trader is given the option to buy a set number of stocks for a set price within a certain timeframe. If the price of the stock increases, they are able to purchase the shares promised at a deep discount and then turn around and sell them off at the higher price for a profit. To visualize this process consider a bargain shopper at a flea market. The shopper comes across a deal that is too good to be true. For $5, the shopper purchases the item, but it is actually worth $50 on eBay. The shopper could turn around and sell the $5 item for $50 and pocket the $45 difference. This is essentially how call options work. You are guaranteeing yourself a price to purchase something at in the future. If you like the price, you can exercise your contract. If you do not, you are just out the money you spent to enter the contract.

Trading at an Inflated Price

Put options are on the short side of traditional options. Rather than buying at a discount, the trader is selling at an inflated price. With a put option, the trader acts as the seller of the shares, with another party promising to purchase, hopefully at a price higher than what they are currently worth on the market. The trader, during a successful trade, has the opportunity to sell the stock they hold for a price much higher than the market price. If you purchase a put option contract, you are looking for the price to drop. The higher the strike price of the put option, the more you are able to sell the shares for, meaning more earnings for you. For example, assume you pay a movie rental company $5 for the opportunity to borrow your favorite DVD. You then return to the flea market in the above example and sell that same DVD for $20. When it comes time to return that DVD, you will want to find a cheap replacement so you can make as much as possible off of the transaction. If you can find a copy of the DVD to return to the rental company for $5 at a store, you will have made a profit of $10. This might seem deceitful in this context, but within the stock market, it is a perfectly acceptable, and extremely profitable, practice.

What separates these two types of trades? In both, you are buying and selling something. Just like traditional short sales, the difference is in the order that you do so. You are not initially purchasing the DVD in the put option example; you are paying a premium to borrow it. The buying does not occur until the DVD becomes due to the rental company. This is how covered options work. As you will soon see, there is an alternative to actually selling shares that you own. The bid price and the ask price are the two numbers that market makers look to when fulfilling an order.

Market Makers

A market maker is a trader who facilitates trades for corporations, funds, and individual traders and investors. These market makers are a rather large reason why markets perform so smoothly.

The difference between the bid and the ask price is known as the spread. When it comes to call options, you are usually buying shares at the ask price and selling at the bid. The bidding price is the highest price that someone is willing to pay for the stock, while the asking price is the lowest price that a seller is willing to part with their shares. With a put option, you will be selling shares at the bid price first, and then buying at the ask price. The bid is lower because this is the price that a buyer wants. In order to get the best deal, they will want to get their shares at the lowest possible price. The ask price is higher because the corporation issuing the shares will want to maximize their profits. The following chart is a hypothetical snapshot of Medifast Inc.'s bid and ask price:

MEDIFAST INC. (MED)		
Club	Bid	Ask
$30.58	$30.49	$30.60

While the spread in the Medifast example is only $0.11, the lower the price of the stock, the wider the spread will be percentage-wise in order to encourage a higher volume of trading. For example, if the stock is valued at $1.25 per share, the spread might be $0.25. Because of this, an interesting opportunity arises. Arbitrage is when a stock is purchased at the low bid and sold immediately at the higher ask price. A trade can be turned around immediately for an instant profit of a few cents per share. If the amount of shares traded is high enough, the commission and fees incurred can be overcome. With options, the spread is generally larger than with a traditional buy or sell. The savvy trader can use this to his or her advantage and create a nice profit.

Put options provide a type of protection that traditional short selling cannot. Because options are not mandatory trades, the trader is never obligated to execute the position. For example, if you were to put a contract for 100 shares of Priceline.com (PCLN) for $200 per share only to see shares rise to $225, a normal short position would be out $2,500. With a put option, on the other hand, there is no need to execute the trade. The trader would then be out only the fees and premiums paid for the opportunity to carry out the option. Because the preceding example would be a trade operating at a loss, the individual owning the put option contract would not want to execute it.

We can take the deal-finding, flea market shopper situation one step further. Rather than purchasing the item, bringing it home, and posting it on eBay, assume the shopper simply sold the item without actually purchasing it. This is how a naked put works. The trader will sell stock that he or she does not yet own with the hope that the amount they are paid will cover the amount of money owed to actually purchase the shares plus a profit. Naked puts, also known as uncovered puts, are not to be confused with naked shorts. Naked shorts are considered illegal and are monitored by governmental institutions. With no capital actually invested, individuals participating in a naked sale can make an infinite percentage of gain since they are in essence never in ownership of the stocks they short. With put options, this does not present a problem since the trade need not be executed if the trader feels they will be unable to complete the deal. There is a much lower degree of risk associated with naked puts because of this.

The ups and downs of put options

Put options, if used correctly, have several advantages over taking a traditional short position of the same company's stock. For one, there is less risk of capital. You do not need to invest as much with a put option as you do with a short sale because naked puts are not illegal. Therefore, you would only be out the contract price of the naked put option since you do not necessarily need to purchase and provide the shares in question unless you actually decide to exercise the option. Furthermore, if it looks like you will need to cover your position, you have the entire length of the contract to purchase the shares, allowing you to pick the optimum price at which to buy the shares. You also have a much higher degree of leverage with put options than you do with a traditional margin account. In a margin account, your spending power is merely doubled.

With a put option, hedging your investment becomes much simpler and cheaper. By straddling your position, you are essentially taking a stand on both sides of the trade, the long and the short. This works best with highly volatile stocks since the hope is that the market will sway far enough in one of the two directions in order to make the trade profitable. Obviously there are fees and commissions for both sides of the trade that need to be overcome. If you are not sure of what direction you think a stock will go, yet you are convinced that when it does move, it will move big, straddling the option, although it can be expensive, is your best choice.

The main disadvantage of a put option is time. Because stocks fall at a much faster rate than they rise, time is a friend to traditional short sellers. The longer that they hold on to the short sale, the more opportunities there are for the stock to drop in price. The reverse is also true. The longer that a position is held, the more time there is for the stock to rise. Make sure that you have a firm idea of where the stock's future is headed prior to initiating a position.

Time also causes the price of a put option to decay, and eventually expire. If the stock you option has not significantly dropped prior to the expiration date, your put will become worthless since there will be no point in exercising the contract.

Types of Put Options

There are two main types of put options that need to be discussed. A covered option is an option that you write using shares you already own as collateral for the trade. Traders use this type of option to hedge against losses and maximize earnings. Instead of a trader paying his or her broker, the premium money would go to you, the seller of the option. Should the price rise above the strike price, making the trade profitable for the person on the other end of the trade, you would receive the original premium minus the gains the trader generates as you transfer the stocks you already own to the holder. Even if the stock in question drops in value and the holder chooses not to exercise the option, you as the writer of the option will gain the premium costs. In this case, it is a win-win situation for you.

On the other hand, **naked options** contain a higher degree of risk. With a naked option, you do not need to actually possess the shares you are guaranteeing at the time of the writing of the contract. Because stocks fluctuate in price, writing a contract for shares you do not yet own can be dangerous as you will need to provide those shares should the holder wish to execute his or her contract. When it comes time to provide those shares, the price may have turned for the worse. This does not mean one should avoid naked options. They can be extremely valuable to the brave trader since they give a very high degree of leverage within a trade. When you write call options, your profits are cut by the price you pay for the shares you will be providing. This cost disappears with a naked option, allowing you to maximize profits. Still, this type of trading requires great amounts of discipline and intestinal fortitude.

This should not be confused with the naked short selling of stock. Naked short selling shares of stock is an illegal practice. The options market is slightly less regulated, allowing for this similar practice to be completely legal. Although very risky, this type of trading has the allure of extreme rewards.

Naked options are a bit different than their covered counterpart. If a contract expires worthless, you are netting pure profit from the contract premium. You never need to worry about actually owning the promised shares. The worst thing that can happen to a trader selling naked put options is that they will have to supply the shares at the contract rate. The best way to handle this is to only sell put options of stocks that you firmly believe in. This way, your options trading will resemble your own trading philosophy; you will be selling shares that you would have bought anyway.

The Mechanics of Writing Options

Being the writer of an option is a much different world than being the holder. With writing options, there is a much greater degree of risk due to the fact that the decision to exercise the contract is no longer yours. The holder, whoever enters the contract with you, now is making that decision. Because of this, many brokers will require that you have at least $25,000 in your margin account. If the worst happens and you need to cover your position because of an exercised contract, you may need this amount (or more) to prevent a default on your part.

When you take part in writing a call option contract, you are selling the opportunity to purchase shares of a stock to another trader at a later date. As stated above, you can either already possess those shares as with a covered option, or you may not own those shares yet, as with a naked option. Either way, the mechanics for beginning the trade are relatively similar. First, you will collect the premium from the other trader. The various factors that influence fees are discussed in the next section.

Once the premium is collected, there are a three things that can happen:

- The stock will fall in price
- The stock will remain unchanged
- The stock will rise in price

Only with the last occurrence will you be responsible for actually executing the option contract. With the other two choices, it makes no sense for the call option contract holder to execute their contract; they would be losing money on top of their premium if they did. When you are the holder of a call option contract, the odds are stacked against you. You will lose money if the price drops or stays the same. The only way to make money is if the price goes up. Two out of three of your final possibilities with call options end in you losing money. This changes when you begin writing options. Now you are making money if stock prices drop or stay the same. You are only losing money if the price of the stock goes up. And as we have already established, a rise in prices takes much longer to occur than a dropping off. Writing a call option is much easier to make money off of than holding a call option for this reason. If you put in the work doing the proper research for your stocks, you have a quite good chance of being rewarded with a profit.

Suppose the worst does happen and you end up with a stock rising in price and the holder exercises their option. What happens to the writer? In this worst case scenario, you will be responsible for providing the appropriate amount of shares. If you have written a naked call option, then you will be responsible for buying the shares for the holder, regardless of the stock's current price. If you were to find a struggling company that is selling shares for around $1.00, you might decide to sell a call option contract of 100 shares to another trader for $0.50 per share at a price of $3.00. The beleaguered company, instead of dropping in price as you imagined it would, declares that they have just secured a new funding source and suddenly their stock jumps in price. Soon, the stock is sitting at around $5.00 per share. Rather than pocketing the earnings and never looking back, you now have to provide those 100 shares to the holder. Instead of a small profit of $50, you now are looking at a much larger loss of $450 ((100 shares x $5 per share) -

$50). While the holder gets a discount of $2.00 per share, you are paying $4.50 per share to secure that price for the holder.

Factors that Influence Fees

Options are not free; they definitely have a cost associated with their contracts. As with any trade, a fee or commission must be paid in order for the trade to be executed by a broker. This fee is given as a per share price, with 100 shares being the typical minimum amount per contract. With options there are four main factors that influence premiums.

<u>Strike Price</u>

The strike price is the price at which an option contract is to be executed. It is agreed upon by both parties and is binding to the providing party. For example, a put may have a strike price of $100 per share. Even if the price drops to $50 per share, the writer is obligated to purchase the shares at the higher strike price of the $100, assuming that the holder wishes to exercise the contract. The more favorable the strike price, the higher the associated fee will be. The holder would only want to execute their option if the price was above the current market price. This way, a larger profit would be realized than if the stock was just shorted on the traditional market. With put options, the lower the strike price, the cheaper the contract. This is because with a put option, you will be selling the shares at the given strike price.

The strike price is the ultimate determining factor in whether the option is going to be profitable to the trader. Of course there are also nominal fees associated with option contracts, but if the difference between the current market price and the strike price is great enough, the fees will be easily overcome. An option that is going to be profitable to the trader is referred to as being "in the money," while an unprofitable trade would be considered "out of the money." A breakeven trade is said to be "at the money."

Expiration Date

The daunting term "expiration date" is simply the last date at which the option contract may be executed. An option can be carried out at anytime in between the commencement of the contract and the expiration date. The longer the time period before the expiration date, the more valuable the option is. This is due to the fact that there is simply more time for fluctuations within the price of the stock. Once the expiration date passes however, the option becomes worthless if it has not been acted upon.

The easiest way to visualize how an expiration date influences the market price of a put is to think of the price as the way the trading public views the future of the stock in question. For example, if there are six months left before the expiration date of a put contract, and the market price of your contract is $1 more per share than the current price of the stock, the market is expecting the price of the stock to drop by $1 over the course of the six months.

Ease of Obtaining

Also known as liquidity, the ease of obtaining the shares in question plays a large part in the determination of the fee for the option. If the broker has a difficult time finding shares to cover your position, the price is likely to be much higher than if there is an abundance of shares. A situation like this might occur if you are looking to trade a stock that has a very low volume. Option clearinghouses such as **www.thinkorswim.com** facilitate the trading of options and have greatly helped in making them cheaper to obtain, but this rule still applies. Large-cap stocks will prove to be cheaper to take a put position with than small-cap stocks just because there are more shares available.

<u>Risk</u>

The risk, or volatility, of the stock is the last factor in determining an option's price. The more volatile the stock is, the more it is going to cost since the chances of it fluctuating to a favorable price are much higher, especially if there is a long period of time in between the start of the contract and the expiration date. The standard deviation of a stock is one method of quantifying risk. Standard deviation essentially measures how spread out a stock's prices are. For a stock that typically trades within a tight range, the standard deviation will be small. On the other hand, if the stock experiences large gains and losses throughout the course of the trading day, it will have a much larger standard deviation. By this manner, a stock's pricing history can be evaluated and future price patterns can be predicted.

Put option pricing

The strike price and the expiration date are the most quantifiable of the factors influencing price per share. Assuming that you are looking to purchase a put option on Jan. 1, the pricing schedule below illustrates how time and dollar amount influence prices.

STRIKE PRICE	EXPIRATION DATE		
	January	June	December
$82	$6	$8	$10
$80	$3	$5	$7
$78	$2	$4	$6
$76	$1	$2	$3

So, if you were to purchase a put contract with a $78 strike price that has an expiration date at the end of December, you would pay $6 per share for a total of $600 — since an option contract is generally for 100 shares. This does not include any additional fees that your broker would charge. As you can see from the above chart, the higher the strike price, the more of a fee you will incur for a put with a consistent expiration date. You will also notice that the further away the expiration date is, the higher the fee since there is more time for the stock's price to change favorably for the trader. In the above example, if you were to exercise this contract, there would be a total of $7,800 returned to you, or 100 shares at $78 each. Not bad for a $600 investment.

While the chart above is just a simplified example, the actual process of determining option fees is a rather complicated process. The most common method is known as the Black-Scholes option-pricing model, which takes into account current stock pricing, the strike price, expiration date, and volatility factors such as standard deviation and risk-free return. These factors, although complicated, work together in the influence of options pricing. By becoming aware of them, you will be better able to spot when an option's price is reasonable, thus making your trade that much more likely to be a successful one.

Measuring Volatility

It is one thing to say a stock that is being optioned is volatile; it is another to actually quantify it. Just because a stock jumps up and down in pricing does not necessarily make it a good short sale. Over the years, mathematicians and market experts have devised ways to actually put a number to the degree of volatility that a stock might carry. These are especially useful when purchasing put options since volatility plays a large role in the pricing schedules that options brokers use. Greek symbols are used for the naming of these measurement tools. Vega, although not technically a Greek symbol, falls under this category.

Delta (Δ) signifies the rate of change in the option's purchasing price in comparison to the stock's price. Both the sensitivity and the volatility of the stock are taken into account with this measurement. Delta ranges are from 1 to -1 with 1 meaning that the call option is far out of the money and -1 meaning that the put option is far out of the money. The extreme numbers are for options at their expiration date. An easy way to think of option pricing is that for a delta of -0.5, a $1.00 price increase in the stock will affect the option's pricing by a decrease of $0.50.

Theta (Θ) is the measure of the amount of time that is left in the put contract. This essentially measures the rate at which an option contract will decay per day. Time as an element of price sensitivity is measured here. Theta is a theoretical indicator of the change in value from day to day as the option nears its expiration. In order to achieve this calculation, the contract's time is measured against real time price changes within the chosen stock. For instance, a theta of 50 means that the underlying value of the option will decrease by $50 per day. This is because options are finite trades; you can only exercise them up to a certain point.

Gamma (Γ) compares and contrasts the delta of the option and the stock's price. Basically, it ventures to quantify the time-to-price sensitivity. A high gamma indicates that the option is far from its strike price. However, gamma does not take into account whether an option is in or out of the money. It only states the distance from the strike price, regardless of whether it is above or below that given price. So a high gamma is not necessarily a bad thing.

Rho (P) stands for the option's contract value versus the interest rate. The interest rate sensitivity is thus determined. With a rho of 10, with each percentage point the interest rate changes, the options price is altered by 10 percent, depending on if the interest rate moves up or down.

Vega (Y) takes into account how much an option will change in price when the underlying security changes by 1 percent. Vega can also change even if there is no change in the stock's price. This would be the case if the volatility of the stock were to increase.

There are several other mathematical terms that describe the volatility of an option, the foremost of these being beta. **Beta** is a term that compares the movement of a stock to the flow of the overall market. If a stock has a neutral beta, it moves perfectly in sync with the market. Low betas move less and high betas move more than the market. When looking at a stock's beta, there are two things to consider. A high beta is going to move more drastically, and thus more quickly, than the market. If you are looking for a quick gain, the higher betas are the way to go. The second thing to consider is that low betas, although they move more slowly, are cheaper. In theory, a beta of 1.1 indicates that the stock is 10 percent more volatile than the market. Remember that volatility is also a determining factor in an option's fee schedule; the higher the stock in question's beta, the more expensive it will be to enter a position. Because of this, you will want to take into consideration both high and low betas when forming your portfolio. It should be noted that beta can be used to measure stock volatility regardless of whether it is being optioned or not.

Keys to a Successful Put

The advice for carrying out a successful put is going to sound familiar; just because you are dealing with options rather than a straight short sale does not make much of a difference in how you execute your trade. Still, there are some key points that should be emphasized.

Patience

The necessity for patience cannot be overstated. There are literally thousands of trades out there; you just need to find the right one. Once the right trade is found, it is just a matter of timing it correctly. How long do you predict you need before the stock plummets in price? Remember, the timeframe of the put is a key component in its fees; if you think your trade requires a longer amount of time before you will be ready to exercise the position, you might want to consider waiting in order to save money on fees. Shorter options will have a much more attractive price tag.

Use Your Capital

While options create opportunities for more leverage than a traditional short sale, they still lock up your money for a period of time. If you are considering buying a put option for greater than a period of one year, think again. Before you lock money up for a long period of time, consider your options. Can that money be put to better use somewhere else?

If you have money just sitting in a put option while the stock in question's price is staying at one place or within range that makes it not worthwhile to exercise, your money is not working for you. An option does not necessarily need to be exercised within a few weeks of initiation, but it should be used within a few months. You should only buy an option if you suspect that a price reversal is coming up soon. If your money is left to stagnate for longer periods of time, this is money that is not making you more money.

Follow the Leaders

Institutional investors such as banks, insurance companies, and mutual fund brokerages all have major influences over the price of stocks due to the simple fact that these entities control very large percentages of company shares when compared to individual investors. If these powerhouses are beginning to leave long positions within a sector or a particular company, you can almost guarantee that as demand for the vacated drops, prices will too in order to try and attract new investors. You will want to be there on the short side when this happens.

Capturing profits

Part of the allure of put options is that they can easily multiply profits — when used successfully. This can be accomplished in a few different ways. The first of this is by **pressing** your investment. Pressing your investment involves cashing in a successful put option, and then reinvesting the principle amount and any profits into a new contract for the same company. This would be the case if the stock has reached the price you originally thought it would sink to, but something occurred that makes you think that it will continue to decline in price. There are a few instances in which this would occur.

- The stock is still at an unsustainably high price but has not yet begun to drop.

- The company is fundamentally flawed, and there are at least two months before the expiration date in the new contract.

- The stock is in a freefall.

- New indicators have come to light showing that the stock in question is going to sink even lower.

Another method of multiplying profits would be to **rollover** your investment. This is a bit more conservative than pressing and involves setting aside profits and reinvesting solely the principal amount. In this instance, once you choose to exercise your option contract, you would reap the profits and set them aside for future trading or whatever other purpose you deem fit. The amount that was initially used to purchase the first contract would then be recycled in order to buy a second contract. This allows you to risk less money while still taking advantage of the great opportunity that option contracts allow for. These methods can help multiply profits in a way that traditional short selling cannot. For example, assume you purchase a put option contract, or 100 shares, of Apple Inc. at a strike price of $210 per share. The stock currently sits at $200.

With an expiration date three months in the future, you might be spending $10 per share. Based on your research, you think the stock will fall to $190. If everything works out in your favor, and you exercise your contract, you will be paying $1,000 in fees, but gaining $2,000 for a total profit of $1,000. But assume you still believe that the stock has further to drop. Again, you buy another put option contract at the $210 strike price. When the stock drops to $180, you gain another $2,000. If you were to have shorted this sale, the most you could have expected to make is $2,000. But because you were able to roll over profits and reinvest them into the put option contract, you were able to increase the money you were to make by 50 percent.

General warning

Because of the lesser amount of risk associated with options, they sometimes attract individuals with small bankrolls and little experience. Options are dangerous for beginners because they decay in value over time. Take a look at the following example:

Jodie has been watching Green Mountain Coffee Roasters, Inc. (GMCR) and believes that they will drop down to $70 per share. Jodie picks up the put option at the current price of $81.13 — earning herself a profit of $11.13 per share. She plans on buying one full contract, with the hopes of profiting $1,113. The stock does exactly what Jodie imagines it will, only it does not do so in a timely manner. Jodie purchases an option with a two-month expiration date; by the time the stock finally plummets, the two months are over. Jodie was exactly right about everything to do with the stock and would have made money had she just sold it short. But because options expire, Jodie has lost out.

The need to understand a stock's Greek symbols is important in the above example. If Jodie truly understood everything to do with the factors that make an option decay in value over time such as the Greek symbols, she may have waited to short GMCR, or she may have just sold the stock short. Regardless, a missed opportunity can be expensive. The contract for GMCR would have cost a little more than $400, giving Jodie a profit of $713 had the trade gone off like she expected ($1,113 - $400 = $713). Instead, that $400 now belongs to her broker.

Another occurrence that merits a word of warning is the fact that it is vital to find your own trades. What this means is that if you simply follow the crowd while trading options, you are not going to be making as much money had you found new and unique investment opportunities.

Chapter 10

Exit Strategies

People always want more. Greed is a powerful motivator within the stock market. It will also drive people to end short trades too late as they wait and wait for stocks to drop even further. What often happens in reality is that stocks will have started to correct themselves and a good chunk of the profits previously made are lost. Ironically, greed causes people to gain less in this instance. There are a few scenarios that you must be familiar with before you begin a trade, and knowing when to exit a trade is one of the most important parts of trading. After all, how are you supposed to collect your earnings if a trade remains open indefinitely?

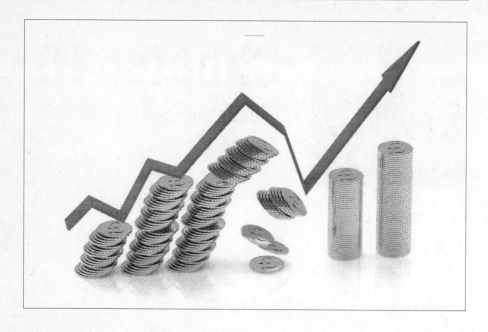

Setting Safeguards

Before setting an entry point into a short sale, you need to set an emergency exit point. This should take into account both a price that you do not want the stock to reach and the general turbulence of the market. While you do have complete control over when to enter, when you are exiting a sale it is subject to the whims of the market. A stop-loss point should be secured, whether it be an automatic one that you pay your broker to establish or one that you impose yourself. Either way, this point should be located at a place where you do not expect prices to go. Of course you enter a short sale in order to make a profit because you do not expect any trades to lose you money — otherwise you would not enter them. But markets do oscillate, and your short sale will seldom move in a straight line. Your stop-loss point should be a price a tiny bit above where you can realistically expect prices to rise to given the oscillating nature of the market.

Setting a stop-loss point is a great way to limit the degree of risk your trades face. When a trade betrays you and goes where you do not want it to go, safeguards will protect you. Both market orders and limit orders will allow you to walk away from your computer and not worry about stocks rising while you are not paying attention.

A market order is a much more expansive type of order, but they are not always given top priority. Market orders are filled after a specific price is reached but not always in the timeliest fashion. If you have a short sale that you entered when prices were $20 per share, and you have set your stop-loss point as a market order at $21, the price might be filled at $21 or maybe not until the stock has reached $21.50. It is even a possibility that the price can go even higher before the order is finally filled. On the other hand, limit orders are much more exact and are better at avoiding the slippage that occurs with market orders. However, because they must stipulate an exact price, it is possible a stock could miss the specified price range. Because of this, limit orders work much better as entry points because they guarantee that you will enter a position exactly where you want to.

Whether you are using actual stops by paying your broker to establish them for you or you are picking a number that you will exit the trade at and sticking to it, discipline is a vital part of setting safeguards. You need to be strong enough to set them before entering your trade and then have the tenacity to adhere to them once you are in the midst of things.

Most of all, it is important to feel comfortable with the trades you make. Your trading diary will encourage you to return to past trades and reevaluate them. But do not be too harsh on yourself. It is very easy to identify patterns and trends when you are looking at a chart from a trade you made a month ago. It is another thing to identify these patterns when you are currently trading. You cannot regret a trade, even if the price of the stock in question plummeted after you covered your position. Tell yourself that again: *You cannot predict the future.*

When you trade without regrets, you are trading in a more cerebral fashion. You are using your intellect rather than your emotions. Regardless of what may have happened to the stock after the trade was over, if your trade was made according to the guidelines you set up for yourself, your trade was a successful one. Even if it was a losing trade, it was a learning experience. This does not mean that your emotions should be completely discounted. You can use your emotions to your advantage. For instance, if you have a string of losing trades, you might feel upset about them. You can use that anger to better yourself as a trader. Take some time off from the market and study the trades that lost you money. If you find an analytical error that you were making and correct it, your emotions have spurred you on to become a better trader.

Profitable trades

Although we expect every trade to be profitable (Why else would we enter the trade in the first place?) realistically we must admit that this is impossible. Before a trade is initiated, a plan needs to be put in place so you can easily secure a profit and reduce the chance of losses.

A target profit price should be established and written in your records before the trade begins. This says where you will feel comfortable taking your profits and walking away from the trade. Because it is unlikely that the stock you choose is going to drop in price down to zero, you need an exit strategy for when you will be satisfied with your profit margin and call it quits. True, this does mean that you will oftentimes end a trade too early. Stock prices rarely act in the manner we envision them acting. You will sometimes see prices continue to drop after you have recovered your position. This is simply an inevitability of the market. Remember, as a short seller, you are in the business of making money. If you short a position and you exit it at your stop point, it is true that you might be losing out on a small portion of the profits you could be making, but you need to remember that the stop point was chosen for a reason. If you carefully plot out your decisions and do not just arbitrarily put your money in the market, you will have nothing to worry about.

It is important to note that by selecting an exit price for profitable trades, you will be creating a secured and guaranteed profit rather than holding a position for too long. If you are lucky, you will be chasing your losses at 80 percent of the top price, but a much more likely scenario is 50 percent. Your odds of being closer to the top on your original exit point are much better than trying to rush to close a position after stock prices have already begun to rebound.

People are seldom happy with the status quo. Life can always be improved upon and trades can always be made better. So what do you do if you are in a profitable trade, and it looks like the stock is going to continue to drop in price? Despite the rules that you set for yourself, you will need to factor in room for error. These changes should not occur often, but there are always exceptions to the rules. Maybe something about the stock or the market conditions has changed, making you rethink your goal exit price. If this is truly the case, you are allowed to prudently edit your trading strategy. However, this does not mean that you should always do so. There has to be an exceptional argument to be made in favor of the changed trading strategy. You chose your original exit price for a reason. You should honor that price in the vast majority of instances. Remember, it is better to get an early profit than it is to get a loss later.

Losing trades

Ending a losing trade is one of the hardest things to do in the trading world. We enter each and every trade because we think that the short sale will be a profitable one. We should always have a degree of surprise when a trade proves to be unprofitable. That does not mean that we should not be prepared in this event.

Remember how an unprotected short sale can, in theory, lead to an infinite loss? We do not want this to happen. Whether you are a day trader and are receiving constantly updated stock prices every few minutes or you are a position trader checking your short sales a few times a day, you do not want to trade without some sort of protection strategy in place. You can achieve this in a couple different manners: checking your trades constantly or instituting a stop-loss point. For day traders, the first option is not a problem as long as they remain disciplined, but for the more casual trader, the latter is going to be a necessity.

A stop-loss order is a market order that will automatically close a short position once the price of the stock in question rises to a certain point. The stop-loss point should always be a price at which you do not expect the stock to attain; if the stock rising in price does not surprise you there would be no point in executing the trade. If you fully expect a high stop-loss point to be reached, wait to execute the short sale until it has reached the higher price. You will save yourself much money with this strategy. Most on-line brokers will provide stop-loss points for you at an added cost. While some types of traders will not need this type of pro-tection, most will enjoy, and minimize their losses with, the extra safety that it brings. Peace of mind is not an easy thing to come by in the stock market, and although it comes at a price, you should seriously consider this safety net.

The type of trading that you are planning on partaking in will partially determine where to set your stop-loss points. If you are a day trader, your stop-loss points need to be much closer to the beginning price than if you were a swing or position trader. This is the case because of the speed in which decisions need to be made when you are a day trader. A day trader must make a much quicker decision than the position trader simply because of the amounts they trade and the manner in which they trade them. Think of it this way: Because a day trader is looking to make quick profits off of the market, they trade more money so that they may take advantage of small gains and losses within the market.

Again, there are exceptions to the rules you have created for your-self. If you absolutely must change the exit price, do so by mov-ing the stop-loss point closer to your original entry price. Never move it away from the entry. This may mean that you need to re-enter the trade at a later point if you still think the stock is worth short selling. Usually this will not occur for quite a while after you end your trade, though. Even professional traders take advantage of this option; no trade is off limits as long as it shows the promise of being profitable.

Trades stuck in limbo

When a stock just does not want to go up or down in price, it might not seem like a big deal. But the more money that you have tied up in one trade going nowhere is less money that you can be putting to good use. With each and every trade you should be marking in your trading journal how long you think that it will take for the given trade to materialize and how long you are willing to wait for it. If a trade seems to be stuck in limbo for too long, you need to end it. This is largely determined by the type of trader you are and the goals you have set forth. For instance, a day trader may think that four hours is too long to have a trade open, while a position trader might hold a trade open for several weeks before they think the trade has lost its value.

Your money and your time are both valuable assets, wasting them is not doing you any favors. When you have your money tied up into a trade going nowhere, it is money that could be better used somewhere else that actually makes you money.

Determining exact stop-loss points

How do you know exactly which price to use as a stop-loss point? This is a tough question and can be answered in as many ways as there are different trading styles. In other words, there is no set in stone method of setting your stop-loss points that is universal from trader to trader. However, there are a couple key factors that need to be considered.

- How comfortable are you with the volatility of the stock in question?

- What do you consider an acceptable amount of oscillation?

For example, if you are looking to short shares of Apple Inc. when it reaches $230 per share, you will need to determine exactly when you should abandon your position if the stock does not act in the way you think it will. The first thing that you should look at is Apple's normal ups and downs. For this, you will need to look at a daily chart, as shown below:

As you can see, the chart for Apple appears to have a resistance level right above $230. A resistance level is a price that the stock just cannot seem to go above for quite a period of time. Unless this stock breaks through that resistance level, the stock will probably not go much above $230. Trading psychology plays a large role here. It might not make sense that a stock will not continue to rise unless it reaches a certain level, but when traders see a stock within a definite trend (breaking through a resistance level would be the start of a trend in this instance), more and more traders will jump at the opportunity to get on a winning trade, forcing the price to rise even more. If you look at the daily high you will see that the price has stalled out at $230.20. A stop-loss point of $230.50 might be appropriate in this instance. This will allow you to take advantage of the stock's sudden rise, while allowing you to exit the trade if the price does the unexpected. It is not recommended that you set your stop-loss point only a few cents above the most recent high. As you may remember from the double top and head and shoulders patterns discussed earlier, it is possible for a stock to retrace a recent high repeatedly before falling. By setting your stop-loss point too close, you will be actually losing money that you otherwise could be saving if you only stuck with the trade a bit longer. Try to look at about 0.5 percent above the previous high when setting a stop-loss point. This number might vary slightly depending upon the volatility of the stock, however.

There is another method that gives traders a more exact answer. There is software out there that will determine at exactly what price you should initiate and end trades at. Trading programs can be bought through your broker or through outside private companies hoping to capitalize off of trader inexperience. These software programs are not recommended because they do not take all factors into account and do not provide for the wiggle room that comes with determining trades on your own. These programs do not have an advantage that we as human traders possess: psychological knowledge. We are able to look at companies with upcoming events such as earnings releases and new products and can gain a better understanding of how others will respond. This is something that is not only vital, but also impossible for computer programs to take into account.

Still, for traders who are just starting out, checking to see how closely your numbers fall in comparison to a program's numbers can be a good way to check your work. If your numbers are in agreement with the program's, this can be just the boost of confidence needed for the kickoff of an excellent trade.

Patterns for Exiting a Position

 There are several patterns that indicate that the ride is over and the short sale needs to be covered. One of the most prominent of these is the **cup and handle** pattern. This pattern mimics just what it sounds like: a large dip in price (the cup) followed by a recovery and then a less pronounced dip (the handle). Here, stock prices will drop, forming the left-most side of the initial decline in prices. Then the stock will start to rally, only to drop again, this time in a less severe manner. When the price begins to rise once again, this is an indicator that the stock's bear run is over. More often than not there will be a breakout in the stock's price as it rises more consistently. If you look closely at this pattern shown below you may see a now familiar formation. The cup and handle is a variation of the head and shoulders pattern that takes place on the bottom of a price chart rather than the top.

The **bullish harami cross** is another indicator that a decline in price is about to reverse. This pattern is apparent when there is a wide trading range that ends far down for the day. This is followed by a narrow trading range that ends up for the session. For technical traders, this is a clear signal that a trend has come to an end and you should cover your position.

The **bullish homing pigeon** is an indicator that tells us that the current bear trend is coming to an end. This consists of a large downward trending candlestick followed by a second smaller downward trending candlestick that is completely engulfed by the first one. The important factor within this candlestick chart formation is that the first day of falling prices that is represented is done so in a strong fashion, whereas the second downward trending day is much weaker. This can be taken as a signal to cover the current short position as the trend has come to a temporary end.

A **bullish abandoned baby**, despite having a morbid name, is a strong signal that it is time to close your short position on a stock. This signal takes the place of a strong downward trending day followed by a small gap down where the following day has a very slight trading range that is also downward trending. The third day is a very strong gap up day that ends with a large gain for the stock. If you have not covered your position prior to this signal, there is a strong suggestion to do so afterwards. The stock's price has begun to climb again, you do not want to be stuck with a losing trade. The bullish abandoned baby pattern is also known as the **morning star** pattern and is the exact opposite of the previously discussed evening star.

While these signals are not accurate predictors one hundred percent of the time, they are established as being right more often than not. Practice will help you identify these patterns more immediately and allow you to look at a wider array of charts in a shorter period of time.

Chapter 11

Testing the Waters

B y now you should have a firm grasp on what a short sale is, how they work, and what to look for before and after executing a trade. You should also be familiar with the several variations of a short sale and the level of risk that each one entails. This section will walk you through a sample trade, from beginning to end. Not only will we practice how to scan charts, but we will walk through determining a stop-loss point, identifying a safe and profitable exit point, and go through a post-sale analysis including grading the steps of the sale. Strengths and weaknesses will be addressed here, giving you an idea of pitfalls that may occur in the heat of the moment. This chapter will conclude with a checklist of common things to look out for when you are trading on your own.

Scouting Trades

A time-tested strategy for scouting trades for a short selling day trader begins the night before. You should have in mind a few stocks that you are looking to trade whether it is information from the evening news, the newspaper, or your online discussion group. Have a good three to five companies in mind and look at the weekly chart for each of them. We will be looking at the weekly chart first to get a sense of overall trends within the stock. If these look promising, we will then move onto daily charts for more accurate interpretations. For the sake of this experiment we will look at three stocks: Overstock.com (OSTK), Apple Inc. (AAPL), and Green Mountain Coffee Roasters (GMCR). Overstock.com was recently selected by Yahoo! Finance as a stock that has a high rate of bearish traits. Green Mountain and Apple were chosen because they have been recurring stocks throughout this book. The past week's charts are all included below, complete with superimposed price channels and volume charts.

Overstock.com

Overstock.com's chart is a prime example of a short sale candidate. There was a large gap up on Wednesday, March 31, as the stock broke through its upper price channel in drastic fashion. As the channel and the price readjusted to the new higher prices, the stock slightly fell in price only to continue upward shortly after. Take a look at the chart below:

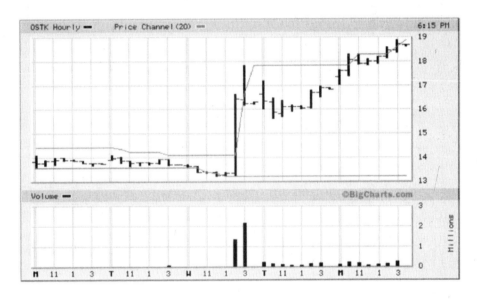

There are a few clues that make this stock a great candidate for a short sale, the most glaring of these being its extremely low volume in comparison to the gap up that took place on March 31. This stock is also beginning to show the classic double top pattern. As you know, it is possible for a stock to retrace itself before plummeting down to the short seller's glee. The low volume here only reinforces this. This stock also appears to be eager to burst through the top of its price channel, a pattern that is unlikely to be sustained. If the opening price is at or near its high, this will be considered a very promising trade.

Apple

Apple has proven to be an extremely interesting company as we have looked at it throughout the course of the book. The recent release of the iPad has given the stock quite a bit of media attention, causing for an increased volume of trading and a boost in price. Take a look at the chart below:

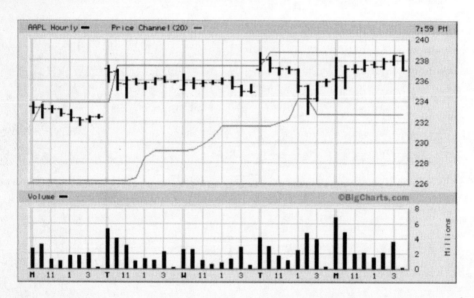

There are a few things that stand out about this chart. The most obvious being that the price bars have been at the top price channel for almost the entire five days. Normally, this would be an anomaly, but the iPad has created media frenzy around the trading of this stock. A stock normally does not sustain a price this high for this long, but Apple has certainly accomplished this, as it has been pushed upward by a steadily high volume thanks to the release of a new product.

This stock, although it looks to be operating at an unsustainably high price, is probably going to stay up near the top of its price channel for the next several days. The high volume, coupled with a new product release, do not bode well for those looking to sell Apple short. Because of these reasons, we will abandon the short sale of Apple, at least for the time being.

Green Mountain Coffee Roasters

Green Mountain Coffee Roasters stock has also risen steadily since the middle of 2009. Sometimes, even over the course of a week, the stock would rise by $8 or more. The chart for the past five days is below:

This chart differs quite a bit from the first chart we looked at for Overstock.com. Rather than a steadily rising chart at the upper portion of the price channel, we see here a stock that has been oscillating regularly and is actually now near the bottom of the price channel. What this stock does have in common with the Overstock.com chart is the low volume. This stock has been moving sideways for the past day and a half and with the sudden drop off in volume, looks like it is poised to move downward.

Plotting Your Next Move

Once you identify which stock(s) look enticing enough to act upon, you need to decide how you will approach them and how you plan on exiting the trade. We have trimmed our list down from three stocks to two (Overstock.com and Green Mountain Coffee Roasters) that need to be watched during tomorrow's trading day. As you grow more experienced, the number of stocks that you can handle on any given day will increase; largely, it will be left up to market conditions to determine which stocks and how many of them you will trade with.

Now we need to decide where we want to set our entry and exit points. We also will need to decide how many shares we wish to short. This number will be determined by the size of the bankroll; for this example, assume this number is set at $500,000. One percent, an appropriate entry point, of $500,000 is $5,000. We can double this number due to the leverage gained by our margin account so we will be trading with $10,000 total. Because Green Mountain is a more expensive stock, naturally we will not be able to short as many shares. The stock closed at $96.94, so it is safe to say we will enter Green Mountain at just above $97; we can, with a degree of certainty, set a limit order for $97.10 to enter our position. This will give us a bit of wiggle room in case the opening price is not what we expect. A good, but ambitious, exit point for a profitable trade would be a price that we are quite certain that the stock will drop to over the course of a few hours: $95.95 seems to be safe and attainable. With $10,000 set aside for our entry point, we can safely short 100 shares of this stock. A drop of $1.15 per share for 100 shares gives us $1,150 profit. Our stop-loss point will be set at $98.25 since this is safely above Monday's daily fluctuations. This is a price where we do not believe the stock will actually go, and it is also not so low as to be a price that will occur within the previously attained range of trading.

Overstock.com closed the trading session at $18.68, 20 cents below its high point for the day; $18.88 also happened to be the high point for the year. If this stock is going to drop like we think it is, $18.73 is a good spot to start our short sale. $10,000 will get us 530 shares of the company; for the sake of simplicity we can round this number down to 500. Our goal exit point can be set at $18, as this stock appears to be quite volatile. If the stock rises to $20, we will abandon the trade as a lost cause, and 500 shares falling $0.73 each will give us a profit of $365.

As these are day trades, we will not be holding positions over night. If the stocks do not reach the prices we set for them, we will simply abandon the trade a few minutes before the markets shut down for the evening.

As many of our case studies have informed us, before we enter a trade, it is important to get a feel for the overall trend of the market. Both Overstock.com and Green Mountain Coffee Roasters are traded within the NASDAQ Composite Index. The weekly chart for this index can be seen below.

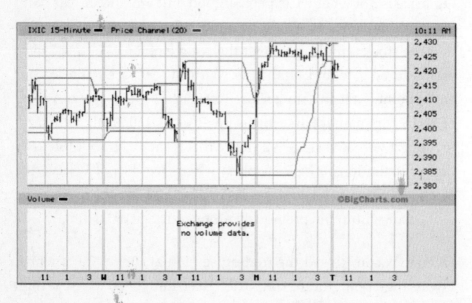

As you can see, this index rose quite a bit at the end of last week to the beginning of this week. There was a gap up that occurred early Monday morning prior to the index leveling out for the remainder of the day. Its price channel significantly narrowed after this occurrence as the standard deviation caught up with the sudden change in price. It appears that the index is going through a period of minor ups and downs. As we are day trading, this should suit our purposes well.

We bought Green Mountain Coffee Roasters near the opening for the day at $97.28. This is our entry point to the short sale. Our profit margin can be modified from $1,150 up to $1,330 as we entered the trade at a higher price than originally intended, and we are keeping our exit price of $95.95 the same.

Overstock.com opened and fell to an unexpectedly low price of $18.15 within five minutes of markets opening. This is a little low for our purposes, we will have to hope that the stock jumps in value before plummeting a second time. Shortly after the opening bell, Overstock.com's stock spiked to $19.24. This will be the entry point for our short sale as we were a bit late with our order. We will be maintaining our stop-loss at $20, and our ideal exit point at $18.00. Our new profit margin it $620 for a successful trade.

When Stop-loss Points are Hit

Green Mountain Coffee Roasters meet its stop-loss point around 11:15 a.m., not even two hours after the markets opened. A sudden gap up brought the price from $97.75 up to $98.40 with a buyer purchasing 600 shares of the stock, a trade six times as big as the one we were acting on. Because of this large trade, the price of the stock saw a dramatic increase. The gap up can be seen on the far right of the chart on the following page

As you can see from the information provided, gap ups are sometimes impossible to predict. It appears that this trade is over for the time being. Perhaps we might be able to try it again before the end of the day if the charts warrant the trade.

Shortly after Green Mountain Coffee Roasters hit its stop-loss point, Overstock.com reached a price of $19.90. It seemed that this stock is going to continue on its way up, so the trade was abandoned at this price.

As you can see from the chart above, the double top pattern that we originally saw never quite materialized. Instead, the price line continues to increase.

It turns out that abandoning the Overstock.com trade early was the right decision. By covering our position sooner than originally planned upon, we ended up saving ourselves money. Remember, if you are going to change your plan, only change it by moving the exit price closer to the starting price. Ten minutes after the stock hit $19.90 it climbed up to $20.25. By leaving the trade early, we saved $50. This brings the total loss for Overstock.com to $330. Add that to the loss of Green Mountain Coffee Roasters, and we have a total loss of $427 for this round of trading.

Because of Overstock.com's normal volatility, we were not quite to abandon the trade. When the stock showed signs of dropping again, we reentered a short position at $20.25 for another 500 shares. Take a look at the chart on the following page:

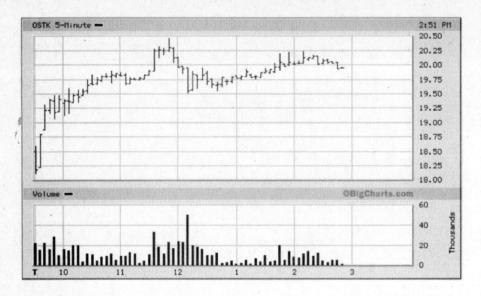

In all probability, the stock would drop to just above $19.50, so I set a buying order for $19.55. When we reenter the trade, we need to set new stop-loss points. The highest price hit for the day so far was $20.46. At this point, it might be tempting to set our stop for that amount, but remember that we do not want to have it too close to the top of the chart because this time, there might be a real double top. Instead, we will set our stop-loss for $20.60, a price that we will be realistically surprised to see.

When the stock dipped to $19.95, we jumped at the chance to secure a small profit from the trade and covered the position. At a drop of $0.30 per share, this trade had a net profit of $150 bringing our daily total to a loss of $277.

Wrap-up and Analysis

This example of a short selling day trader's thought process leading up to a sale and throughout the course of a day was intended to give you a taste of what trading is really like. Markets will sometimes not act in the manner you think they will, as was the case with Green Mountain Coffee Roasters, so you will lose some money, especially when you are just starting out. As stated previously, short selling can be likened to a form of art. It is only with practice that you will master it.

By grading the three trades made over the course of the day, we will learn where areas of weakness were and improve upon them. Remember, we assign multiple grades to a trade: an entry grade, an exit grade, and an overall trading process grade. We will also see our strengths, and be able to further capitalize upon them. We entered the Green Mountain Coffee Roasters trade at $97.28 and we exited when the price hit our stop-loss point of $98.25 for a loss of $0.97 per share. Let us look at the stock's statistics to see how we stacked up.

OPEN	HIGH	LOW	CLOSE
$96.50	$99.17	$96.50	$97.66

There were two instances where the stock brushed with $99 early on in the day. The second of these, in retrospect, would have been the most appropriate place to enter. Again, we see here a typical double top formation that is built up and then comes tumbling down all in the course of one hour. Shortly after the high of $99.17 that occurred later in the day also would have been an appropriate entry point as volume dropped after the build up in price; but again, it is easier to know what to do with a trade in retrospect. As far as a grade for the Green Mountain Coffee Roasters' entry, it would be an F. The entry point was closer to the bottom of the chart than it was to the top. Exercising a degree of patience and allowing the price to increase a bit before entering would have been a much better course of action.

Seeing as how our exit was the result of a stop-loss point being reached, there is no need to grade the exit; we did exactly what we should have according to the plan. Overall, however, this trade earned a D. Even though it was a losing one, because of sticking to the plan and exiting the trade when it became clear that it was going to be unprofitable, the trade was not the disaster it could have been.

Another thing that could have been improved with this particular trade was the reward-to-loss ratio discussed Chapter 1. The actual reward to loss ratio here was 1.2:1, which is a bit on the low side. Remember we should have been aiming at a ratio of at least 2:1.

Overstock.com climbed to its 52-week high during the course of the hypothetical trading day, but we were still able to have one good trade with the stock. The intricacies that day traders look for are often overlooked when looking at weekly charts, but even during the course of a very fruitful day, a rising stock will have slight dips. If you are savvy enough to find them, you can make quite a bit of money selling the stock short. Look at the finished daily chart for Overstock.com:

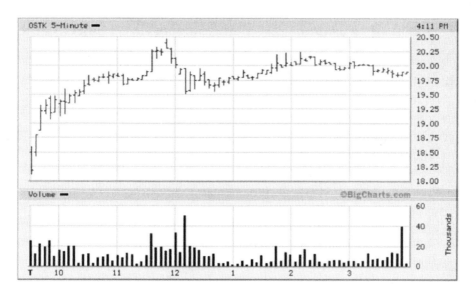

There were two places where selling this stock short would have been profitable, we were able to latch on to the last one that began just after 2 p.m. Unfortunately for us, this area of profit was much smaller than the drop that began just before noon.

OPEN	HIGH	LOW	CLOSE
$18.50	$20.46	$18.12	$19.87

We will start with the first trade of the day with Overstock.com. We entered at $19.24, again a price closer to the bottom of the chart than it was to the top. This entry also gets an F. This stock was on a roll today, so it would have been much better to let the chart fill out a bit before jumping into a trade, regardless of how well-thought-out the trade was. Each trading day is a new and separate day. Yesterday's prices are history; it is very important that we be aware of this.

Our exit from the trade was well informed. We recognized that the stock was going to be rising for a while and got out before too much damage was done. By moving our stop-loss point closer to the original entry point, we saved money. The total loss on this trade was $330 and the reward to loss ratio stood at 1.9:1, just shy of our 2:1 goal. The overall grade of this trade was a C+, thanks to the quick thinking that ended the trade early.

The second Overstock.com trade fared much better for us. Although we did not recoup all of the losses from the previous two trades, we were able to heal our bankroll and our pride. We entered this trade at $20.25, for once a trade that occurred near the top of its chart. This made the entry was a B+. Our exit was close to the closing point at $19.95, an A- exit that netted a profit of $150. Ironically, this trade, although profitable, had the lowest reward to loss ratio of any of our trades at 1.2:1. The overall trade was an A- despite this.

For the day, we lost $277. While we were hoping for a gain, it was definitely not bad given the potential losses that we would have faced had we not operated with stop-loss points in place. And by documenting the thought processes that created these trades, we will be able to learn from our mistakes and improve upon them for the next trading session.

The Rundown to Shorting a Position

Selling stocks and other nonequity financial instruments short has great potential for making money regardless of what the market is doing. While there are many factors to consider before entering a short sale, with a bit of knowledge and the willingness to learn even more, you too can become a successful short seller. There are many signs that indicate that a short sale should definitely be executed. Some of these include:

- The market is in a confirmed downward trend. It is difficult (but not impossible) to make money shorting stocks when prices are going up across the board.

- There should be a degree of volatility. Stable, blue-chip stocks do not have violent drops in price.

- A realistic opportunity for profit appears. You should genuinely believe that a stock would drop 20 percent or more. Even if the stock does not actually drop by this much, the opportunity for it to do so should be apparent.

- A particular sector appears to be contracting. This will usually be the one that benefited the most from the past bull market, such as dot-com bubble in early 2000s.

- Overhead supply becomes apparent. The most recognizable instance of overhead supply is the head and shoulders pattern. When a stock is rallying but having trouble going back to its former trading range, it is a good indication that the stock is poised to fall in value.

With these factors for entering a trade in mind, there are also some factors that should be recognized that indicate you should *not* enter a trade. These include:

- Markets have been in a bearish trend for more than two years. Stocks take longer to recover than they do to fall, but typical recessions do not last more than two years.

- A stock keeps hitting new highs. Despite what you think about the stock in question, there is no limit as to how high a stock can rise. Even if you think it is overextended, you should wait until there is a noticeable signal that the stock is going to drop in price.

- A stock has gotten a lot of hype. Just because many analysts have recommended that you short a particular stock does not mean that you should do so. Sure, maybe the analyst on television boasts of having a 75 percent rate of correct picks, but this is not a clear-cut indicator that he or she will be right this time. You need to do your own homework.

Selling stocks short adds a valuable weapon to your trading arsenal. Not only can you profit when prices rise as traditional investors do, you can profit when they fall. By learning to effectively sell short, you are increasing the opportunities you have for making money. A savvy investor can find upward trending stocks even in the worst bear market, but it is difficult. Selling short during a bear market is more efficient.

There are many mistakes that new short sellers make. Some of these can be easily corrected, while others are considered to be major setbacks. Perhaps the biggest mistake that new traders make is not keeping a trading journal. This has been mentioned several times throughout the book, but it remains imperative. The necessity of taking notes regarding your trades is so important that you should probably stay out of the market altogether if you do not plan on keeping some sort of journal. The market is so big, and you will make so many trades that it will be impossible to store everything you learn within your memory. By keeping some sort of trading notebook, you greatly reduce your odds of making errors in the future. Other common pitfalls include:

- Trying to time a short position right at the peak of a stock's price. Although this would prove to be extremely profitable, it is impossible to determine when a stock has hit its peak in real time. Instead, you should wait for sell signals to occur before entering a short sale.

- Getting emotionally involved. The higher your degree of tilt, the more likely you are to make errors. Trading when you are excited about a recent gain or trading when depressed over a recent loss are equally detrimental. Do not take losses personally: Learn from them.

- Chasing losses. If you are losing money in a trade, do not make a rash decision that may end up costing you even more. If you experience a great loss, take notes, rest for a bit, and then get back in the market refreshed.

- Changing stop-loss points. If you must change your stop-loss points, do not change them so that you have more leeway. Stop-loss points should only be adjusted toward your goal price. This will end up saving you money over the long run by getting you out of poor short sale choices much earlier.

- Not paying attention. If you are not serious about excelling in the market, it is not worth your time or money to get involved. When you execute a trade haphazardly, odds are you are going to get burned.

Many techniques and practices will make you a successful short seller. Chief amongst these, as mentioned before, is the keeping of notes. Others include,

- Study. Read books on trading and short selling. Take notes on them so that you can better retain the pieces of information you collect. Read financial newspapers so that you have a better understanding of the overall economy and how it is affecting the companies that have captured your attention. Pay attention to the news as well.

- Be prepared. There are many different variables within the stock market. While it is impossible to be prepared for all of these, it certainly is in your best interest to be prepared for most of them. A good trading platform, broker, and strategy will help you here.

- Develop a system. Whether this is a mechanical process or a discretionary one, you need some sort of structure to your trading. Only time will tell what works best for you, so pay attention to what benefits you, and get rid of the practices that do not. It does not matter if you plug numbers into a computer to generate trades or you do it the old-fashioned way as long as you pick a system and stick to it.

- Use both styles of analysis. Most short sellers rely solely on technical analysis and chart patterns. While this can be beneficial, you will be multiplying your chances of success by confirming trades with fundamental analysis as well.

- Play to your strengths and improve upon your weaknesses. Just as a professional athlete uses his or her best skills during an actual game and then at practice works on weaknesses, you should be honing your weaknesses during non-trading hours and using your best skills when it comes time to trade.

- Use averages. Exponential and simple moving averages are powerful and simple technical indicators. These can be modified and used with almost any trading strategy, ranging from day trading to long-term investing.

- Wait. If you are unsure of a trade, there is no harm in waiting. There will always be more trades just like the one you passed up. The stock market is vast; if you are not 100 percent confident that a short sale is going to be profitable, do not waste your time, money, or energy.

Great traders are not born overnight. By practicing and improving upon the craft of trading, you will learn how to maximize profits and minimize the inevitable losses.

Conclusion

Short selling is not a widely accepted practice, but this does not mean that it is a negative or detrimental one. On the contrary, short selling is a valuable tool within markets, allowing them to function easily and facilitate sales between different entities. Because short selling is so mysterious, it gives those that truly understand what it is and how to use it a huge advantage when it comes to making money. Rather than only profiting on one side of the market, you are now able to profit on all sides.

Selling short does not need to be a mystery, though. The practice has been around for centuries allowing contrarians and hedgers to profit during some of the worst market times. With a bit of practice, you can easily master the mechanics and be able to identify the pieces of a successful trade. There is truly a type of short sale out there for everyone, if they only knew where to look.

The type of trader you are does not matter. Both fundamental and technical analysts alike can use short selling to help supplement their portfolios. These distinctions have each been discussed in lengths with the hopes that you will be able to pick and choose from each one in order to find your happy medium.

Is selling stocks and other financial instruments short a worthwhile practice? For many, the answer will be no. Most people either do not have the time or choose to use their time differently when it comes to studying the markets and choosing where to place their money. Because you made it this far in this book, you are not like those people. As long as you are an active student regarding the market and put in the necessary time, you can and will be a successful short seller.

In order to make short selling work, you need to be vigilant. A large part of trading entails conducting research and waiting for your picks to hit the prices you want. With many beginning short sellers, there is a tendency to rush trades, to enter or exit a trade too early. Your best bet is to remain patient and attack trades on your terms. There are not many things that you can control with the market, so the parts that can be controlled should be used to your full advantage. The most important thing aspect you can control is your entry price. Once you enter, though, your degree of control quickly dissipates. The more in control you are, the more likely you are to have a profitable trade.

Short selling might be controversial, but it is a proven way to make money because markets both rise and fall in price. By only buying and selling in the traditional manner, you are cutting your earning power in half. Ask yourself this: would you be happy if you were making only half the money you could at your place of employment? The answer to this should be a resounding no. So why not take advantage of all your money-making potential?

Appendix

This book has included many resources for where to turn to for more information. Below, you will find a compilation of these sources, including reference materials that were used in the construction of the book.

Internet Sites:

http://finance.yahoo.com: Yahoo!'s Web site devoted to everything financial. This is a great source for scouting out companies that have earning reports coming out soon.

www.bigcharts.com: A charting package that allows you to customize your own charts, picking the indicators that are most important to you.

www.etrade.com: A discount online brokerage.

www.investopedia.com: A source for market news. This site also has a great online dictionary for financial terms.

www.investors.com: The Web site for the newspaper Investor's Business Daily.

www.marketwatch.com: A Web site that contains market news and updates.

www.scottrade.com: A discount online brokerage.

www.sharebuilder.com: A discount online brokerage.

www.stockcharts.com: An online charting package. This is one of the more sophisticated charting packages, allowing you to design charts with indicators of your choosing.

www.thestreet.com: An online news source for market updates.

www.thinkorswim.com: A discount online brokerage that specializes in options trading.

www.wsj.com: The online home of The Wall Street Journal.

Newspapers:

Financial Times

Investor's Business Daily

The Wall Street Journal

Glossary

A

Accumulation/distribution: A formula that shows any discrepancies between a stock's supply and its demand. It does this by looking at price trends compared to the trading volume.

Arbitrage: The practice of purchasing something and then immediately selling it in a different marketplace for an immediate profit.

B

Bankroll: An amount of money set aside strictly for trading.

Bankruptcy: A legal process declaring that a company is unable to pay its debts.

- **Chapter 7:** This type of filing indicates that the company cannot be saved with judicial intervention.

- **Chapter 11:** Also called a reorganization, this type of filing necessitates having a judge appointed in order to oversee the company's restructuring as it prepares to re-enter the commercial market.

Basket fund: A group of stocks bunched together because of a common underlying theme.

Beta: A measure of a stock's volatility.

Bollinger bands: A technical analysis tool that plots lines over the price chart two standard deviations of the stock's simple moving average away from the actual price. This charting tool can indicate buy or sell signals when the stock's price breaks out of the bands.

Bond: A loan that is taken out from a corporation or government with a promise to repay the principal plus an interest rate to the investor.

Broker: A licensed individual or group that is legally allowed to conduct securities trades for others.

Bubble: These occur when a sector of the market is traded at an extremely high price in comparison to the actual value of the companies within the sector. When bubbles pop and prices correct themselves, there is the potential that the entire sector or market will be brought down with it.

Buy in: The broker's right to recall shares of stock borrowed for short without giving advance notice.

C

Candlestick chart: A method of charting changes in price created by Japanese rice traders. This type of chart displays the most amount of information in the smallest space.

Capital gains: A special tax paid by people who profit from the stock market. Currently, the rate stands at 15 percent but will revert to 20 percent in 2011.

Commodity: This term incorporates any item that can be traded that is non-equity based. Examples of commodities include livestock, oil, food products, and gems.

D

Debt/equity ratio: A fundamental indicator that shows how much a company owes versus how much money has been invested by shareholders. A high debt to equity ratio may mean that the company is not fiscally healthy.

Derivative: See "options."

Dividend: An agreed amount that is paid out to shareholders per share owned. Companies are not required to pay out dividends but many do in order to reward their shareholders.

E

Earnings per share: A fundamental analysis method that shows how much profit per issued share a company has made. This usually covers the company's last four quarterly earnings reports.

Envelope: A set of two bands over a price chart. When a price reaches these bands it triggers a buy or a sell signal.

ETF sponsor: A company or financial institution that compiles an ETF for public trading.

Equity: 1) A stock. 2) The amount of actual capital left after margined dollars are subtracted from the account.

Exchange-traded fund (ETF): A basket fund of like companies that trades like an individual stock.

Expiration date: The date by which an option must be finalized or its contract becomes void.

Exponential moving average: A momentum indicator used by technical analysts. The closer the unit of time is to the present, the more importance it is given.

F

Foreign exchange (forex): The world's largest marketplace. Billions of dollars worth of international currencies are traded each day as people travel or conduct business with other nations.

Free riding: The act of finalizing a trade before the initial selling of the stock is finalized. This can be avoided if sufficient funds are available in your margin account.

Fundamental analysis: The act of looking at a company's inner-workings in order to determine whether the company is a good candidate to open a position with.

Futures: An agreed upon contract that forces an individual to buy or sell a commodity on a given date.

G

Greek symbols: The Greek symbols measure the effect of time and changes in price on an option's fee schedule.

I

Index: A compilation of stocks that are put together in order to measure a portion of the market's overall health.

Indicators: A signal that shows some aspect of a company's overall health. This can include both fundamental and technical indicators.

Inflation: The process by which a currency becomes devalued.

Insider trading: This is said to occur when an official or someone with inside knowledge of a company conducts a trade of that company's stock. Illegal insider trading occurs if an insider conducts their trade without announcing it beforehand or if they act upon nonpublic information.

Institutional investor: These account for the majority of dollars traded within the U.S. stock market. These investors include banks, insurance companies, and fund managers.

Investor: An individual or company that buys stock with the intent of holding the shares for a sustained period of time in order to make a long-term profit.

L

Leverage: A term for the amount of spending power you have in regards to how much physical capital you have.

M

Margin: A type of account that allows you to borrow money and shares from other traders. A margin account is mandatory for short sellers.

Margin call: A recall of the stock's borrowed from a broker. This can occur at any time, but usually only if the broker sees uncertainty that may jeopardize the shares of stock that they allow to be borrowed.

Market capitalization: The relative size of a company. This is determined by the formula: Number of shares issued X Price per share.

Market maker: An individual who facilitates trades for a particular company or exchange. Market makers account for a large portion of buying and selling within a given venue in order to keep markets flowing smoothly.

Market order: An order to buy or sell a stock at the current market price.

Momentum: The direction and the force with which a stock's price is moving.

Moving Average Convergence/Divergence (MACD): A momentum indicator that attempts to predict when a price reversal is about to occur.

Mutual fund: A group of stocks, bonds, or other equity instruments that is closely overseen by a fund manager in order to fulfill the goals set forth in the fund's prospectus.

N

Naked short sale: The practice of short selling an item that you or your broker do not actually possess. This is illegal when dealing with the stock market.

O

On balance volume: A technical indicator that reflects a stock's momentum. This is calculated by adding a stock's daily volume to a constant when the stock rises in price, and subtracts the daily volume when the stock drops in price.

Option: A contract that gives an individual the right to purchase or sell an agreed upon number of shares of stock at an agreed upon price.

- **Call:** These include optioned shares that are being bought by the individual.
- **Put:** These include optioned shares that are being sold by the individual.

Oscillation: A mathematical term that describes the overall wave-like motion that markets experience.

P

Paper trading: Practice trading with fake money. Many brokers allow you to paper trade prior to actually investing real money.

Portfolio: An investor's complete list of open trades. These include both long and short sales.

Prospectus: A paper or electronic brochure that stipulates the future goals of a particular fund, its past history, and the background of the fund manager.

Price channel: An arbitrary technical indicator that shows the range of the stock's price trend.

Price/book ratio: This ratio attempts to establish a comparison between a stock's trading price and its intrinsic value. The purpose of this calculation is to give traders an idea of whether a stock is at its correct value. Divergences between actual stock prices and theoretical prices can indicate a future price reversal.

Price/earnings ratio: This ratio attempts to show how closely a stock's price follows its actual earnings per share.

Price/sales ratio: This fundamental analysis formula compares the stock's market price to how much the company earns over a given time period.

Projected earnings growth: This fundamental indicator attempts to measure where the company's stock is going to be at some point in the future.

R

Range bound: A stock is said to be range bound when it trades within a narrow portion of its price chart.

Recession: A period of two or more quarters in which the vast majority of the economy has negative productivity. This is usually measured by looking at a nation's gross domestic product.

Relative strength index (RSI): A technical indicator that measures recent gains and losses and shows how they affect a stock's current price.

Regulation SHO: A federal law that prohibits the act of naked short sales when dealing with stocks.

Regulation T: A federal regulation that stipulates how short sales are conducted. Regulation T requires a margin account and also tells how much equity can be borrowed with a margin account.

Return on assets: A fundamental analysis calculation that attempts to show how efficiently a company uses its tangible assets.

S

Shareholder: An individual that owns stock in a company.

Short interest: The interest paid on the stock originally borrowed for a short sale.

Short squeeze: A phenomenon that occurs when many people have sold a stock short. When shares are bought back, the illusion is created that demand is increasing and the stock's price rises in accordance making the trade less profitable for those buying shares back to cover their position.

Simple moving average: A momentum indicator used by technical analysts. All days are given the same significance with this measurement.

Slippage: This term symbolizes the losses that occur with every trade, winning or losing. These losses take the shape of fees and commissions that each brokerage will apply for conducting your trade.

Split: The act of dividing the number of outstanding shares in order to double the amount of shares.

Stochastic oscillator: A technical indicator that measures the momentum of a stock. This measurement takes into account a stock's exponential moving average, recent high and low prices, and the most recent closing price.

Stop-loss: An order for a broker to buy or sell a stock once it reaches the given price in order to avoid further losses.

Strike price: The agreed upon price at which an option can be executed.

T

Tax harvesting: The act of transferring a capital gains loss into a new tax year in order to take full advantage of any stock market losses experienced. A loss can be carried forward indefinitely.

Technical analysis: The practice of interpreting charts of a stock's past performance in order to predict future actions.

Trader: A term that uses length of time trades are conducted in by a specific individual in order to describe their stock market strategy.

V

Volatility: The amount of change that a stock, or other security, experiences. The higher the degree of volatility, the more likely the stock's price is to change.

Volume: The amount of shares traded over a given time period.

Bibliography

Elder, Dr. Alexander. Sell & Sell Short. John Wiley & Sons, Inc.: Hoboken, NJ. 2008.

O'Neil, William J. How to Make Money Selling Stocks Short. John Wiley & Sons, Inc.: Hoboken, NJ. 2005.

Shulman, Michael. Sell Short. John Wiley & Sons, Inc.: Hoboken, NJ. 2009.

Taulli, Tom. What is Short Selling? McGraw Hill: New York. 2004.

www.investopedia.com

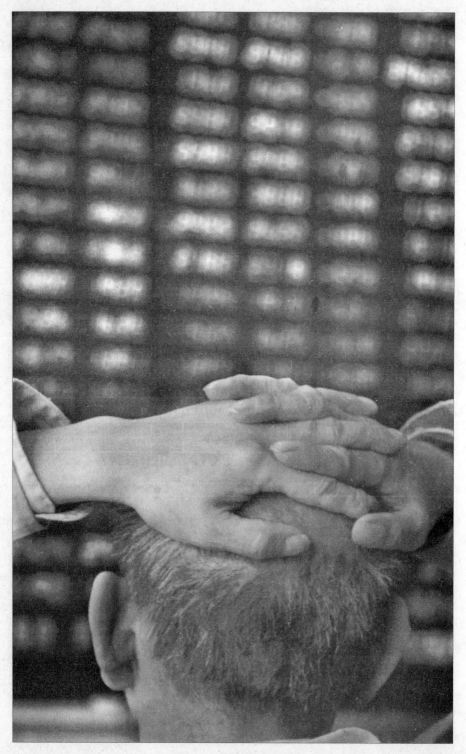

Biography

Matthew G. Young is a freelance writer in Western New York where he lives with his family. This is his second book with the Atlantic Publishing Group.

Index

C

F

Forex, 30, 75-76, 177, 179-184, 186, 192, 264

Forex futures, 182

Forex futures market, 182

Fundamental analysis, 39-42, 254, 97-100, 108-110, 121-122, 152, 189, 264-265, 269, 9

G

Gross national product, 30, 181, 185-186

H

Hedge fund, 57, 59, 183, 191-192

I

Index, 28-29, 242, 118, 133-134, 184, 188-190, 265, 269, 17-18, 2, 11

Measuring Volatility, 213

Money management, 41-47, 78-79, 161

Moving average, 123-127, 129-130, 153-156, 262, 264, 267, 270

Moving Average Convergence/Divergence, 123-124, 156, 267

N

Naked put, 203-204, 206

Naked shorts, 177-179, 203, 9

O

Options, 260, 24-28, 31, 36-37, 75-77, 101, 103-104, 165-166, 171, 177, 188-189, 191-192, 199-209, 211-219, 263, 14, 17, 7, 10

Oscillation, 53, 229, 172, 268, 17-18

P

R

S

Small-cap, 97-100, 114-116, 189, 211

Specialization, 39-42, 45

Spread, 29, 57, 59, 195, 202, 211

Stochastic oscillator, 127-130, 270

Stock shares, 25-26, 63, 65, 14, 17

Stop-limit orders, 38, 40-41

Stop-loss point, 43-47, 49-50, 222-223, 226-228, 230, 235, 241, 243-244, 247-248, 250, 68-69, 71, 82, 84, 103-104, 170-171, 175

Stop-loss order, 227

Stop-market order, 37-38, 40

T

Tax gain/loss harvesting, 50-52

Thinkorswim, 260, 24, 26-27, 78-79, 211

Trading journal, 228, 252

Trading psychology, 41-42, 45, 230, 158

U

W